From My Grieving Heart to Yours

CHARLES W. SHEPSON

ISBN: 978-1-885729-09-5

DEDICATION

To all those
who are groping their way
through the darkness
of the *extension* to the
Valley of the Shadow of Death,
with a prayer that
these shafts of light
that brightened my way
may also cheer
yours.

FOREWORD

The Valley of the Shadow of Death does not *end* when our loved one heads on home! For some it actually *begins* at that point because of the suddenness and totally unexpected nature of the homegoing. For others this valley extends in both directions. It did for me.

From the moment of the dreaded diagnosis of "cancer," my honey and I walked it together. Eight years later that valley ended for my sweetheart, *but not for me*. I still had a long trek ahead of me before I could finally say that I had left that painful valley behind.

I quickly realized that I was not alone, for the same Lord Who had walked with us both up to the point of my sweetheart's death, now kept intimately close to me in my aloneness. There were others there, too! Paul Bubna and Bill Payne walked near enough to me on the trail that, on occasion, I could hear their weeping — and they heard mine. Irene Wiens and Joan Mallow struggled up the same steep slopes that we three did. None of us could hide his or her shortness of breath at times. Nor did we try!

Our momentary encounters brought company and comfort to my heart. Misery does indeed love company, you know! The *right* kind of company, that is! I'd like to keep you company as you stumble through this extension to the Valley of the Shadow of Death. May it please God to have some of these thoughts from my own journal cheer and encourage you, as they did me. Let me know if they help you. That would in turn help me!

Note: Whenever an asterisk (*) appears at the end of one of these devotionals, please read again the opening Scripture text.

THE EVERLASTING ARMS

". . . underneath are the everlasting arms."
DEUTERONOMY 33:27A

"Safe in the arms of Jesus," we sing, referring to our loved ones who have gone "home" before us. But, I am safe in His arms, too! I don't have to wait until my earthly existence is history to claim that position.

Together, during the difficult days, we learned to lean. One of our favorite songs was, "Learning to lean, learning to lean, I'm learning to lean on Jesus. Finding more power than I ever dreamed, I'm learning to lean on Jesus."

But in those days we leaned on each other a lot, too. Now that privilege is gone. I must learn for myself how to lean on Jesus consistently. So, the truth of the matter is that before it was we who were learning to lean (together) upon Jesus. Now I must find out what it means to be "safe in the arms of Jesus" on this side of the Jordan, even as my sweetheart is finding it out on the "other side." It's really not all that different.

For my honey, faith has become sight, but for me *believing* is seeing. "Didn't I tell you that if you would believe you would see the glory of God?" Jesus asked Martha, while she was so deeply grieving. I, too, must believe if I would see the glory of God revealed in this valley of tears.

I will believe. I will not relinquish to my sweetheart alone the joy of resting in the arms of Jesus, and leaning upon them. I don't have to! Those arms are big enough to hold us both, simultaneously — and if we are both in His wonderful arms, then we are not really very far from each other!

Oh what comfort there is in the beautiful statement that *underneath are the everlasting arms*! That speaks of a present reality, a future intimacy and an eternal position. The more I dwell upon that thought, the more comfort it exudes. My sadness is exchanged for gladness; my trials are transformed into triumphs; my aches diminish in His arms; my heartaches are exchanged for "hallelujahs!"

Underneath . . . His everlasting arms!

DOES JESUS CARE?

"When Jesus saw her weeping . . . he was deeply moved in spirit and troubled . . . Then the Jews said, 'See how he loved him!' "
JOHN 11:33-36

A few minutes ago I began to cry very hard — the words from a familiar hymn suddenly erupted from my memory!

> *Does Jesus care* when my heart is pained
>   Too deeply for mirth or song;
> As the burdens press, and the cares distress,
>   And the way grows weary and long?
>
> *Does Jesus care* when I've said "goodbye"
>   To the dearest on earth to me,
> And my sad heart aches till it nearly breaks —
>   Is it aught to Him? Does He see?

I turned very deliberately to the Bible verse that reads, "Jesus wept." I wanted to read it again to enable my sad heart to respond,

> Oh, yes, He cares; I know He cares;
> His heart is touched with my grief;
> When the days are weary, the long nights dreary,
> I know my Savior cares.
>
> Frank E. Graeff

Only the Lord Jesus Himself knows the depths of my grief. It is a comfort to realize that He does know it fully, and He cares about it deeply. I think of a chorus I used to sing, "Jesus knows, and best of all *He cares*, and I belong to Him." I don't recall how the rest of it goes, but that is really all I need.

When Jesus wept at the grave of Lazarus, it was not for the reason the Jews were thinking. Oh, He did love Lazarus, but that was not why He was crying. He knew full well that in a few minutes He would be bringing Lazarus back to life again, so there was no need to cry over his death. No, Jesus was weeping over the depth of the grief He saw in others He loved. He knew He would be dispelling theirs, but He also knew that He would *not* be dispelling yours and mine in the same way. He knew that almost every Christian would be passing through this veil of tears with little relief in the years prior to His return. He heard in Mary's sobbing, mine! He was weeping for me, and others like me.

Does Jesus care? "Oh yes, He cares! I know He cares! His heart is touched with my grief!"

11

THEY FIND REST

"Those who walk uprightly enter into peace;
they find rest as they lie in death."
PROVERBS 14:32

Sometimes I long to have my sweetheart back with me. I miss her so much. I feel like an amputee! This is not just a wound; it is an amputation! A part of *me* is gone, and I find that difficult to accept.

Yes, I would love to have her back, until I remember how difficult life was for her at times. It was in death that *she found rest* and entered into peace. I would not want to deprive her of that so I could be relieved of my own anguish. I love her more than that.

Instead, I will discipline my heart to remember this passage and will take pleasure in knowing that eternal rest came to my honey in death. I will take joy in the truth that for her it is all glory.

For me it isn't! It would be so easy to prolong and deepen my own grief by slipping into self-pity. I must not do that! I must acknowledge with a fresh understanding the joys of her present state, and not recoil from the mawkish, overworked statement that is made to me repeatedly: "She's in a better place." That's trite, but true. I must revel in the truth rather than being repulsed by the triteness.

It was painful for me to look upon my sweetheart lying there in death — but _she_ had _found rest_. Even while my own broken heart was in anguish, and sleep came to me only by assistance, my honey had entered into _her_ rest. I love her deeply enough to be very glad for her.

I must walk _uprightly_ too. Someday I shall find rest in death, unless Jesus returns and provides me with the great joy of meeting Him (and her!) in the air.

Meanwhile I must take great comfort in thinking of both the peace and the rest that is my sweetheart's portion. She ran a good race. There was awaiting her a "crown of righteousness" that complemented her character so beautifully.

It is no longer a _race_ for her; it's a _rest_! Blessed quietness! Peace indescribable! I take comfort in that. _She has found rest._ *

CRUSHED IN SPIRIT?

"The LORD is close to the brokenhearted and saves those who are <u>crushed in spirit</u>."
PSALM 34:18

Thank you for this promise, dear Lord. It was through my tears that I sought for a comforting word from You, but I never expected it to be so explicit! It reminds my heart again that you know *exactly* where I am in this trek through the Valley of Sorrows.

I need to feel you close to me right now, for I am grieving more deeply than usual. *Brokenhearted* and <u>*crushed in spirit*</u> describe precisely how I feel today. I am not suicidal. I have lots to live for. I am just lonely and weepy. It will pass, I know, but as I think of the depth of the love we had for each other, I cannot help feeling my loss — painfully.

Now You are reminding me of the depth of the love *You* have for me, and I must rest in that and rejoice. I am dearly loved by One Who has always been my very close Friend. You are touched by my feelings, and in Your great love You do something about them.

I have experienced Your closeness and its benefits in the past. I will now again. I thank You for that.

A heart that's broken and *a spirit that's crushed* — that's a pretty bleak condition apart from the fact that You are the Healer of broken hearts and the Restorer of crushed spirits. I do not have to despair. I can busy myself reaching out to others and doing things that count for eternity. Even as I follow such worthy pursuits, You will be carefully, tenderly repairing the break, and enabling my spirit to soar and to sing once again.

Touch me, loving Savior, with that tender touch that restores. Cradle me in those healing arms and hands of Yours. Pull me to my feet again and put a smile on the face of my soul, so I don't have to fear that my mask will slip down when I am in public, revealing the brokenhearted person I am. I am *crushed in spirit*. I admit that. I loved her dearly. I cannot dismiss the memories that bring the tears, nor would I ever wish to! I thank You for these encouraging promises.   *

AGAIN AND AGAIN

"The LORD sent word to them through his messengers <u>again and again</u>, because he had pity on his people . . ."

II CHRONICLES 36:15

G od takes note of me, too, in my troubled condition. He takes pity on me and sends word of His loving interest. <u>*Again and again*</u> He sends messengers who are His servants acting out of *their* love, but also prompted by *His* love.

I have received so many cards and notes from people who care. They have selected them carefully, and they want them to be a comfort and blessing to me.

It is all too easy to read them quickly and then to go on to the next one, without allowing the message that was *sent by the Lord through His messengers* to become the blessing it was intended to be.

I must read my cards more thoughtfully and slowly. I must savor the Scriptures, even when they are familiar. The poetry, though sometimes trite, must be allowed to do its intended work. The love of the person sending the card must be allowed to flow freely through that expression of loving concern, serving as a balm to my wounded spirit.

I will take a different approach to the incoming mail the next few days. I'll open and read the card first. Then I will read it aloud as I attempt to extract every bit of sweetness and encouragement from it that I possibly can. I will remember that the cards and phone calls that come to me so regularly are certainly words from my loving Lord, coming through messengers that He is prompting to carry His words of encouragement.

I look forward to that next card or phone call. I am determined to receive it as another of his *again and again* dispatched expressions of loving concern. I will view all of these warm contacts that come my way as personal notes from my Lord. It will make mail time all the more exciting when I maintain that mental stance.

"The LORD . . . sent word to them through his messengers again and again because he had pity on his people . . . "

BOTTLED-UP TEARS

"You have kept my tears in a bottle . . ."
PSALM 56:8

You collect *my* tears? They are precious to *You?* Why, Lord? *Why?* I don't understand that, but I do find it comforting.

If I try to *bottle up my tears* I do myself psychological damage — I know that. I even schedule time for grieving. Crying provides a welcome catharsis for me. I must release my tears!

That's quite a different thing from Your collecting them and saving them. You invented tears, didn't You, Father? You know what man has only recently discovered — that tears are therapeutic and even cleansing. You even made tears of joy with a different chemical composition from grief tears!

I belong to the limited intelligence group, Father. I don't understand much about tears. But You are in that select "Group" of Three whose intelligence has no boundaries.

I attempt to control my tears, but they break through my defenses and spill over my dikes. Help me to accept and even to be thankful for my tears. They are an important part of my grieving. I must not quench them.

Did You save Jesus' tears when He shed them over man's lost condition? Did You save them when He shed them at the grave of Lazarus? I can understand why those would be precious to you. But why are mine? Is it possible that You take a special delight in the love my honey and I had for each other? You said our relationship was a type of the relationship the Lord Jesus has with His church. So when the relationship is as precious as ours was, is there something jewel-like about the tears that I shed as I feel my loss so deeply?

No, I do not understand this verse, but I do read into it a tender statement of appreciation for the significance of my tears. I tend to wipe them away. You collect and preserve them! Will I someday have an opportunity to discuss them with You, going back over the planned circumstances that produced them?   *

RIGHT OF REFUSAL

"... my soul refused to be comforted ..."
PSALM 77:2

I don't want that to be true of me. God has special comforts He desires to bring me. Some are quite generic; others are quite exotic. I must look for them and not miss them.

The pleasure capacity has returned enough for me to be able to enjoy classical music. So far the enjoyment of food is another matter, but in time that too will come.

I cannot dictate to God what comforts He should bring to me, but I can be more receptive to the ones He chooses to send. I can train my heart and mind to be looking for and appreciative of the things He does for me.

Instead of reading the caring notes from kind friends just once before throwing them away, I can deliberately read them a number of times. I can respond to a note instead of just receiving it. I can cherish a happy memory instead of only weeping over it. I can rejoice over the precious years He gave us together instead of lamenting the ones we will not be having. I can stop to look at a thing of beauty instead of simply noticing it and then passing by. I can smell the roses and the gardenias.

Yes, I can adjust my attitudes so that I find myself choosing instead of refusing to be comforted. I know that would please the Lord.

All my life I have determined that the difficult things that come my way would make me better and not bitter. It was a deliberate act of my will. This is not the time to change that practice! I must follow through on this "choosing versus refusing" issue.

The alternative is to deliberately wallow in self-pity and to allow emotionally devastating considerations to affect my degree of well-being. I do not like that alternative. I will continue my choosing of better instead of bitter. I will consciously choose to be comforted. I will, Lord, I will!

By Thy grace, I will!

Thank God for Grief

Really? **Really!** How can God expect me to thank Him for grief? It is such a painful thing. I have not been able to say, *"I thank you, Lord, for how deeply I am grieving."* That seems so unnatural and altogether too "spiritual" to be a down-to-earth, real-life, sincere prayer of thanksgiving.

I should have said, "I have not been able to say, 'I thank You, Lord, for how deeply I am grieving'—until tonight!" I have just had a conversation that has made it painful but actually possible to say those words to my Heavenly Father and say them most sincerely. My friend said to me, "I can't put myself in your shoes. I haven't gone down the path you are walking. I can't grasp the feeling, the loneliness, the grief. But I do go my own lonely way. I do know what loneliness is, even though my wife is still living! Even if God should take her from me, I still wouldn't be able to put myself in your shoes." I knew exactly what he meant, for I know that though he has been so faithful and loving to her, she has not responded to him in the same way.

Suddenly I found myself thanking God, not only for my grieving, but also for the *depth* of it. I am glad that our relationship was so precious that the pain of separation is excruciating. I have so many beautiful memories that can never be taken from me.

Oh, *thank You that I am grieving* as I am. Even for this, I can give thanks. For everything, not just in everything. So deeply I appreciate this new insight You have brought to me.

Now, let me use my tears well by praising You for the happy memories instead of pining in my loneliness; by reliving the happy years instead of resenting the pain; by welling up in praise instead of wallowing in self-pity; by not letting my trial overwhelm, but by letting my trust overflow. Yes, I will give thanks — even for my grief!   *

I CAN

"He reached down from on high and took hold of me;
He drew me out of deep waters. He rescued me . . . You,
O LORD, keep my lamp burning; my God turns my
darkness into light. With Your help I can run through a
barricade; with my God I can scale a wall. As for God,
His way is perfect . . ."
PSALM 18:16-30A

"With *Your help I can* . . ." *"With my God I can* . . ."
Yes, it takes a special enabling of the Lord to do
things some days, but that certainly isn't all bad. When I am
strong it is easy to fall into the error of doing things in my
own strength. When I am weak, I am forced to call upon His
strength for my activities. The result is that I learn the deeper
significance of the truth that His strength is perfected in my
weakness.

Looking back over the course of our ordeal, I have to
marvel at the ways the Lord enabled and strengthened. There
were so many victories. We would have loved to have had the
ultimate victory of a dramatic and complete healing. That

didn't happen, but there were a host of smaller victories along the way. They glorified the Lord and encouraged us.

I called them "smaller victories." Were they? The God Who sees so many things differently from the way I do may not consider them smaller. We have learned to lean heavily upon His strength so as to bring order out of the chaos the disease brought. This may be, in His sight, a most significant victory. We had our own way of doing things, and it was good, we felt. When things caved in on us, we had to learn to adapt and to depend wholly upon Him to lead us through the darkness. He did that. We learned we could indeed do all things through Christ Who strengthened us — and with His help we did!

Now I have new barricades to run through, and new walls to scale. By His grace and with His enabling *I can* do it. Yes, *I can. I surely can!*

With Your help I can run through a barricade; with my God I can scale a wall.

WEAK ENOUGH TO GIVE UP

"When I feel <u>weak enough to give up</u>, You know my way."
PSALM 142:3A (BECK)

David's situation was different from mine, but often his words do apply to my heart. There are those who just give up after their spouse is taken from them. I do not want to be among them! I have never been one to just give up, but I must admit that I can relate to David's feelings so transparently stated here.

Martin Luther's lyrics come back to me frequently just when I need them: "Did we in our own strength confide, our striving would be losing." Yes, but I don't have to confide in my own strength. The One who knows my way, knows how weak I feel at times. He comes to my rescue so faithfully.

I marvel at how candid David is. I think that is why I love him so. He allows his human weakness to shine through. When he goes on to say in the next verse, " . . . nobody's concerned about me . . . nobody cares about me," I hear my very weakest moments echoed. They are moments I don't want to admit even to my closest friends, for they are probably indicative of wallowing in self-pity. I have never stooped to that earlier in my life. I don't want to begin now.

In my low moments, I need to quote these transparent words from David, speaking them directly to my loving Lord. *When I feel <u>weak enough to give up</u>, <u>You</u> know my way.* I may as well say them — He knows my thoughts anyway.

When I (along with David) begin to say, " . . . nobody's concerned about me . . . nobody cares about me . . . ," I had better turn to the Lord asking for a new attitude and a recognition that this grieving is getting the best of me.

People *do* care about me. Some of them haven't a clue as to how much I am hurting, but they *do* care. I probably should be telling some of them that I am suffering as I am. Most of them cannot be to me what I need unless I transparently say, "I'm hurting and I need you." Meanwhile, God knows, even when they don't. *

TOO MUCH!

". . . the journey is too much for you."
I KINGS 19:7C

Lord, this journey through the extension to the Valley of the Shadow of Death *is too much* for me. You strengthened Elijah with special manna, angel-prepared. I know You can strengthen me, as well, with Your own special "manna."

You so tenderly cared for Elijah through Your angel when he was depressed and defeated.

> "All at once an angel touched him and said,
> 'Get up and eat.' He looked around, and there
> by his head was a cake of bread baked over
> hot coals, and a jar of water. He ate and drank
> and then lay down again. The angel of the Lord
> came back a second time and touched him and
> said, 'Get up and eat, for the journey is *too much*
> for you.' So he got up and ate and drank.
> Strengthened by that food he traveled . . . "
>
> (I Kings 19:5:b-8a, KJV)

That whole passage speaks to my heart. You care about my depression! You are sensitive to my feelings. The rightness or wrongness of those feelings is not Your primary concern just now. You want to nourish and strengthen me for the journey. Later You will deal with the specifics.

Oh, help me during these days when the journey seems _too_ _much_ for me. Help me to be very much aware of the times when You use one of Your "angels" to bring both nourishment and encouragement. Sometimes I want to turn them away. Thankfully I have accepted invitations that way down deep I did not want to accept. I preferred to withdraw and be alone. But I went anyway, and when I got there, You strengthened me through the fellowship and nourished me through the food they had prepared. Perhaps both the fellowship and the food were manna.

Please help me to realize that You care about me every bit as much as You did about your servant Elijah. Make very clear to me the truth that You have no shortage of angels skilled in the culinary art of baking a special manna — perhaps even the "hidden manna" spoken of in Revelation 2:17!

ACQUAINTED WITH GRIEF

". . . a man of sorrows and <u>acquainted with grief</u> . . ."
(KJV)
". . . a man of sorrows, <u>acquainted with bitterest grief</u> . . .
(TLB)
ISAIAH 53:3

When someone says, "I cannot fully empathize with you in what you are going through; I have never lost a spouse and I can only try to imagine the depth of your pain," I deeply appreciate their honesty and their attempts to understand.

When another expresses, "I know exactly how you feel; I lost my mother a year ago," I think (to myself), *No, you do not know exactly how I feel. There is a similarity but it is not the same. I know I am right. I lost my mother, too, and my father, but the pain was nowhere near as acute then as it is now.*

Jesus was single. He never lost a dear sweetheart like mine. But though He never lost a spouse, He most certainly is <u>acquainted</u> <u>with</u> <u>grief</u>, even *bitterest grief.* He lost one of His best friends, Lazarus. He stood by the grave and wept with Mary over the painfulness of her grief, entering into it fully. He lost a dear cousin, John the Baptist, whose life and ministry meant more to Him than I can imagine. That touched Him profoundly. He lost His Father! The relationship between Him and His Father was like none ever experienced by others. They were one! Now we are getting into what I am experiencing, because my sweetheart and I were one, also! You may be thinking, "When did He lose His Father?" On the cross! It was there that out of the great depths of His grief He cried out in anguish, "My God, my God, why . . .?" No one can fathom the extent of *that* grief!

Oh, yes, my Savior is *acquainted with grief —with bitterest grief*, and He is able to bring comfort to my heart.

The ones who have comforted me the most have been friends who have themselves lost their spouses. I feel comfortable talking with them about my loss. I know they are willing and even wanting to hear what I have to say. But no one has brought more comfort to my broken heart than the *Man of Sorrows* who is so thoroughly *acquainted with grief*, even *bitterest grief*.

NOT OVERWHELMED

". . . this is what the LORD says — He who created you . . . He who formed you . . . 'Fear not for I have redeemed you; I have called you by name; you are mine. When you pass through the waters, I will be with you; and when you pass through the rivers, they will not sweep over you. When you walk through the fire, you will not be burned . . . for I am the LORD your God, the Holy One of Israel, your Savior . . . Do not be afraid, for I am with you.' "
ISAIAH 43:1-5

God never promised me exemption from trial. *"When you pass through the waters . . ."* and *"When you walk through the fire . . ."* are implying that I most certainly will have trials. The comforting promise is that they will <u>not overwhelm</u> me. My loving Lord is in control, even on the darkest of days; even when the fires blaze the hottest; even when the rivers run the deepest. *I am the Lord your God,* He reminds me. My part is to regularly remind my own heart of this, so that the enemy of my soul cannot gain a victory over my mind. There is no river that is going to drown me. There is no fire that is going to burn me. I belong to the Sovereign of the universe. He is caring for my every need and watching over me lovingly and carefully as I struggle through this persistent, painful time of grieving.

As I think back over the days of our trial, I have to acknowledge that the Lord did help us wonderfully. He brought us one encouragement after another: cards, phone calls, food, flowers, etc. Those special blessings that came so steadily were all parts of the loving watchcare of our ever-present Lord. I shall cross *this* river, too, in triumph. I shall not even have the smell of smoke upon me when I come out of *this* fire — by the grace of God, and with the help of God.

When you pass through the waters, I will be with you; and when you pass through the rivers, they will not sweep over you. When you walk through the fire, you will not be burned . . . for I am the LORD your God . . .

I SAW THE LORD

"In the year that King Uzziah died, I saw the Lord . . . high and exalted . . ."
ISAIAH 6:1

During this, the year when my honey has died, I want to *see the Lord!* I want there to come a new, deeper, richer, closer relationship between myself and the Lord. I want a by-product of my terrible loss to be fabulous spiritual gain!

I want to turn to my Lord and learn from Him in such depth that people will have to take note of the fact that I have been with the Lord and that He has faithfully sustained me.

My emotions are raw. My heart is broken. My world has been shattered. My future is missing one of the brightest and most delightful aspects of my past. But in the midst of all of this, there can come a new relationship to my Savior that is more satisfying than it has ever been before.

King Uzziah was a good king. His reign was a pleasure for all those who were godly. Then, suddenly he was gone, and Isaiah must have grieved his passing. Yet Isaiah could say that it was in the year of this good king's death that he had a most beautiful vision of his God. " . . . I saw the Lord . . . high and exalted."

Oh, Father, let me catch a glimpse of Your glory that will be reflected in my countenance so that others will see the beauty of the Lord and not be subjected to my ever-present sense of loss. Let them see my gain, not my loss (with the exception of my closest friends, who are quite willing to share in my feeling of devastating loss).

There are two elements in this verse: a significant loss, and a most significant gain. Without question, the scale is tipped on the side of the latter. In my life, as in Isaiah's, let the scale indicate clearly that my gain far outweighs my loss. Let my coffers be full because I have deliberately taken into them the silver lining from the clouds of adversity that have hung so low on my horizon. I will intentionally center my thoughts on my gains, rather than my losses. *I will see the Lord!* *

EVEN IN DEATH!

*"When calamity comes, the wicked are brought down, but
even in death the righteous have a refuge."*
PROVERBS 14:32

Y es, we do! Thankfully, we do! I am so desperately in
need of running regularly to that refuge just now.
There is a pain that is known only to those of us who go
through this experience of the death of a dearly loved person.
I cannot escape the pain, but I *can* find a balm that soothes it.

For my darling it is all joy. Her refuge in death is glorious.
In fact, it is so glorious that I question whether this is
speaking about her. Perhaps it is referring to me. Hers is
more than a refuge; it is a state of pure joy and eternal
pleasure. *Refuge* is too weak a word to describe her
environment.

For me, the word *refuge* is very appropriate. I need a shelter
from the emotional storms that sweep in with a suddenness
that startles me. I need a protection from the thoughts the
enemy would propose that are akin to his tactics in the
Garden of Eden, such as, "Has God really said . . .?" I need a
safe place where depression cannot bring me down because

of the powerful Presence of my Lord there with me in that refuge.

Yes, I would say that the word *refuge* is a very appropriate word for me, and I am so pleased that God has provided such a refuge, . . . *even in death.*

Nothing is more final than death. Nothing is more irrevocable. And for me nothing was more painful than helplessly standing by while death claimed my loved one. But death cannot rob me of the truth that it was Jesus who *used* death to take her to Himself. *What a refuge!*

The Lord's my Rock, in Him I'll hide. My Shelter in the time of storm. I'm secure whatever ill betide, for I have a Shelter in the time of storm. Yes, Jesus is my Rock in this weary place — my Refuge in the time of storm.

. . . even in death the righteous have a refuge.

DIVINE KLEENEX!

"The Sovereign LORD will wipe away the
tears from all faces."
ISAIAH 25:8

What serendipity to discover, on this of all days, when I feel so weepy, and the tears come unbidden, a verse in Isaiah I never knew was there. It almost sounds like a verse from the Book of Revelation!

What a tender picture is formulated when I read these words thoughtfully: *The Sovereign Lord will wipe away the tears from all faces.* I revel in the contemplation of that.

My spirit is lifted as I realize afresh that my tears touch the heart of God. I am humbled to think that He cares enough about me to pause and stoop to wipe tears from my face. I no longer feel alone. I feel embraced by God, and my heart is beautifully warmed and comforted by that tender, Divine embrace.

It is easy for me to picture my sweetheart enjoying His welcoming embrace. I must meditate upon this verse until it is easy for me to picture myself in those same arms. How wonderful to be there, together! There is no more comforting place than in His arms.

I would not miss the fact that it is the Sovereign LORD who is applying divine Kleenex to my cheeks. The fact of His sovereignty has sustained me through these painful days. I know that He is in complete control and that nothing happens but what He has either permitted or caused it.

In His sovereignty, He plans our lives, including the length of them, and that applies even to the very moment when He finally took my best friend from me (temporarily).

He knows that my bereavement causes me pain and loneliness and tears because I cannot see things as He sees them. So, in tenderness and love, He does the next best thing to revealing His plans and purposes; He gently wipes the tears away from my cheeks.

I must not relegate that fact to the future only. Today I can enjoy that tender, soft, comforting touch of love. *

DON'T LET THIS THROW YOU

"Don't let this throw you. You trust God, don't you?
Trust me.""
JOHN 14:1   THE MESSAGE

How I thank God that I am living in the day of the proliferation of translations and paraphrases! My life has been so enriched by Ken Taylor, and Beck, and Phillips, and Peterson and others. I love Peterson's paraphrase of the familiar, "Let not your heart be troubled. You believe in God. Believe also in me."

Don't let this throw you, he paraphrases. It could. It would, if the enemy of my soul had his way. I read here a reinforcement of what I have long believed — that I play a big part in whether or not a circumstance throws me. My attitudes are very significant. I must repeatedly remind my heart of the fact that I will come through this long valley of grief in triumph. Already my times of crying are shorter, if not less painful. Last night I cried so hard for about a minute, and then fell off into a good long night of sleep. That's a significant improvement.

No, *I won't let this throw me*. I will stand up to my grieving and be in control of it to a certain extent. That's why I deliberately block out some time for grieving. I don't want to feel that my emotions are controlling me. I shall control them — for the most part.

Oh, I am sure there will long be those moments when I am blindsided and something very unexpectedly triggers a flood of tears. Last night it was a note from the head nurse at Hospice. "Elaine was a real lady," she wrote. How could she have known that when we were going together forty years ago, I had lovingly called her "my little lady"?

In other areas the enemy has attempted unsuccessfully to *throw me*. In this one, if my dependence is upon my all-powerful Lord Who lives within me, He will be defeated again. By God's enabling, he will.

I do trust God. I will trust my caring Savior. I will revel in both their love and power, and I will not allow this to *throw me*. That doesn't mean I won't be staggering a bit at times, but there is a lot of difference between staggering and being thrown. *

GOD COMFORTS ME

". . . God, who comforts the downcast, comforts (me) . . ."
II CORINTHIANS 7:6A

There are days when I feel very downcast — I have to admit that. At those times, I must remember this verse and allow Him to do what He is wanting to do for me.

The word *downcast* aptly describes grieving. So much of what we had set our hearts and our love upon has been cast down. No wonder I am among the downcast at times!

When my sweetheart died, my hopes for a miracle were cast down and shattered. I knew what God was capable of doing. I clung to hope as long as I could. So did she. Even when we signed the papers for Hospice, being told that there was not another thing the doctors could do and from this point on the approach would be only palliative in nature, our hearts had not given up hope — not yet. Death cast those hopes to the ground forever.

Because of some serious medical blunders, my confidence in the medical profession was cast down. An oncologist and a radiologist failed us terribly in their approach and even in their diagnoses (to be fair I must note that there were others who were very helpful to us).

My best friend and biggest supporter is gone — so my most precious relationships were cast down. Not only were all these cast down, *I was cast down!*

"Nevertheless" (KJV) *God* who comforts those who are cast down, *comforts me.* Yes, He does! In the most meaningful and gracious ways, He comforts me: by loving phone calls, by encouraging notes and cards, by invitations to be with others, by food someone lovingly prepares for me, by a new and fresh verse in my devotions, by His "gentle whisper" saying, "I am with you, even to the end of *your* days," by a job to do for Him, by an embrace of my spirit so soft and tender that it is hardly noticed. By all these means and more, the *God Who comforts those who are downcast, comforts me.* My spirit rejoices over the thought!

JESUS HAS THE LAST WORD!

"Jesus has the last word on everything and everyone, from angels to armies, He is standing right alongside God, and what he says goes."
I PETER 3:22 THE MESSAGE

One of my dearest friends called today to make arrangements for two of his staff to come to Fairhaven for help. It was good to hear his voice. I dearly love and respect this godly friend.

After his phone call I framed a picture of my darling to give to my sister-in-law. As I was doing it, I began to recall special things Dot had done for my honey — so many of them! I thought of the bowl of raspberries she so carefully soaked in a Clorox solution for twenty minutes and then rinsed in pure water to get rid of the Clorox taste. She brought them to the hospital for her. Elaine's white count was dangerously low, and this was the only way fresh fruit would be allowed. I thought of other things she had done and I began to cry, hard.

The phone rang. I tried to regain control of my emotions before answering. When the caller heard my familiar voice saying, "Good afternoon, Fairhaven Ministries," the caller was very embarrassed. It was my dear friend calling again, but this time by mistake. "I'm so sorry," he said, "I dialed the wrong number. I was trying to call the missionaries we were discussing so I could give them the dates for their stay at Fairhaven. I dialed you by mistake." Mistake? Not really! I confided in him my sudden burst of grief, and he ministered to me. He pointed me to this verse in I Peter that we are considering in this devotional. It thrilled my soul! It was a great blessing to me to be reminded that the Lord Jesus does indeed have *the last word* *on everything and everyone.* That includes me!

He will decide once and for all when enough is enough. He will stop this flood of tears in his own time. He knows how much grieving I need to do, and when the right time comes, He will wipe away all tears from my eyes. I will trust him. I will cry when I need to cry, and I will laugh when I am enabled to laugh. I will serve Him no matter what, and I will rejoice in the truth that "*what He says goes!*"   *

A DEEP-WATER CATCH

"When he had finished speaking, He said to Simon, 'Put out into deep water, and let down the nets for a catch.'"

LUKE 5:4

D*eep water* scares poor swimmers. *Deep water* has been the undoing of some really good swimmers, too. Yet here the Lord is telling Peter to head for *deep water* and there He gives him a tremendous catch that nearly sinks his boat.

How sad when the depth of the water is all that I consider. Deep water has the potential for a tremendous catch as well. When that possibility is ignored, only fear is produced. That truth must be kept in the front of my mind so that I will not be overwhelmed by depth or waves. I must dare to let down my nets as the Master has ordered, finding unbelievably great quantities of grace, of strength and of peace right there in the midst of my *deep water* trial. One of Simon Peter's most memorable catches came from *deep water*. That can happen for me, too.

Lord, keep me trusting Thee day after day,
  Trusting whatever befall on my way.

46

Sunshine or shadow, I take them from Thee,
Knowing Thy grace is sufficient for me.

Trusting Thee more, trusting Thee more;
May every day find me trusting Thee more.
Cares may surround me and clouds hover o'er,
But keep me, Lord Jesus,
Still trusting Thee more.

Avis B. Christiansen

That kind of trust, even in deep water — no, *especially* in *deep water* — will produce a bountiful harvest, meeting my every need. My nets will be full. My little ship will be overflowing with *a catch* it can scarcely handle!

I wonder what kind of fish they caught that exciting day? I know what the names are of some of the "fish" I catch: grace, peace, strength, trust, hope, faith and patience. Some of these "fish" are very rare, too!   *

HE REMAINS FAITHFUL

"Even when we are too weak to have any faith left, he remains faithful to us and will help us, for he cannot disown us who are a part of himself, and he will always carry out his promises to us."
II TIMOTHY 2:13   THE LIVING BIBLE

My faith account seems totally depleted sometimes! In so many ways I am extremely weak. In times like these, I am greatly encouraged to have this reassurance of His solid faithfulness.

Yes, He will help me. He could not disown me, even if He wanted to (and that thought never so much as crosses His mind!) for I am now *a part of Himself!*

God has never, *ever* broken a promise. He is the original Promise Keeper, not Coach McCartney. His word of promise is all that I need. My faith, or lack of it, while sometimes playing a part, is not the deciding factor.

This verse begins with the words, "Even when we are too weak to have any faith . . . " There are times like that — times when others must do the praying for me. But the most comforting thought of all is that God is God, no matter what!

He remains Who He is: loving, merciful, gracious, caring, giving, protecting, benevolent and all-powerful.

Nothing much is constant in this life. The longer I live, the more I recognize that. Because of that disconcerting inconstancy, the changelessness of God is all the more appealing. That *He remains faithful to (me)* becomes an anchor, when my faith is too weak to hold me steady.

Those who have never walked through this valley may judge me for not having stronger faith, or a more steady anchor. God does not. He just stands by lovingly and ministers to me in my brokenness, my emptiness, my emotional and spiritual exhaustion.

At those times, when I feel the lowest, I need to read and reread this wonderful text. I must remember that I am *a part of Himself* and that He will keep every last promise He has made to me.

ANGRY WITH GOD?

"Lord, if you had been here, my brother would not have died!"
JOHN 11:32B

Did Mary speak this in anger toward the Lord Jesus because He did not come in time to save her brother? I think so. She had dispatched the messenger with that tender note, "He whom you love so much is sick." Jesus could have come immediately to heal him of his illness, but He chose not to. He deliberately stayed where He was. That grieved her!

A missionary friend who agreed to read these devotionals and make helpful comments wrote, "I appreciate the absence of a chapter on being *angry with God*. I can't imagine that you were. Disappointed that Elaine wasn't healed? Certainly. But not angry." She was right! I have never had a moment of anger, and in spite of the predictions of some who "know" so much about how grief is supposed to progress, I don't ever expect to be angry. I have a deep consciousness that my Lord loved my sweetheart even more than I did. He loves me deeply, too. He does everything well — everything! I know that. My deep confidence in both the love and the sovereignty of God is holding me steady.

But! I am not critical of those who *do* become angry with God, nor do I feel that they sin by being angry. Jesus did not rebuke Mary for her statements, which I believe were pregnant with bitterness. He simply wept over the sorrows of mankind — sorrows that He would not be fully alleviating. That is, not for a while!

No, friend, there will not be a chapter growing out of my *anger with God*. I have none. But there will be one that lets those who suffer in that way know that their God is so big that His loving arms surround them even when they flail out against Him.

To the one crying out, "I hate God!" I say, "That's OK! He loves you even while *you* are hating *Him!*" To the one who says, "God is either malevolent or He is impotent!" I say, "That's OK, *that's OK!* God is so full of love for you that He can handle these bitter expressions, and keep on deeply loving and understanding you, even in the midst of your anger."

SPECIAL TO HIM

*"You should know that the LORD makes the one He
loves someone special to Him."*
PSALM 4:3 BECK

T here is something very beautiful about this verse,
something *very* comforting. The Lord loves me. I know
that. And since He loves me, I am very *special to Him*. I need
to know that, too.

We felt it was very important for our children to know
that they were very special to us. They are adults now, and I
still feel that way about them.

God knows how important it is to me to feel *special to Him*,
too. And I do. I *really* do! When I stop to think about all the
ways the Lord has blessed and helped me, I *know* I am *special
to Him*.

I was very special to my sweetheart. I deeply miss having
someone to whom I am extra special. So now I must let the
Lord fill that gap in my life. What a great privilege it is to be
special to the Lord of the universe!

Lord, You are special to me, too. I mean that from deep
within my heart. Some people would feel that you don't really

52

need that at all, but I remember that You said that You were looking for people who would worship You in spirit and in truth. I believe it means a lot to You, too, when Your children specifically state how special You are to them.

You created me needing to feel special to someone, Lord. In this verse I hear You promising to more than fill that big hole in my chest.

David said, "You should know . . ." Yes! It is very important to know how _special_ I am _to You_, and even to rehearse that truth repeatedly until I recognize what a special position I hold in Your great heart.

When I truly _know_ that I am _special to You_, I am profoundly comforted. I find a new song coming into my heart, where there has been no song. I find sunlight bathing a path that has been dark and gloomy. I find myself rejoicing where there was only sorrowing.

Yes, I am _special to You_ because You have loved me dearly and have made me special. I bask in the warmth and beauty of that truth. *

THE TIME HAS COME

". . . the time of the singing of birds is come."
SONG OF SOLOMON 2:12   KING JAMES VERSION

When I am alone, I find myself extra emotional just now — I am approaching a tender anniversary. This morning Stan came to my door. I think he saw the remnants of the tears in my eyes — *so did Jesus!*

The Lord Jesus took the time to make this a special day for me, filled with unanticipated beauty. I will reminisce here over just one of the serendipities with which He filled this special day, turning it into a colorful one!

While talking to Stan's wife a few minutes ago, on my portable phone, I suddenly gasped! *"Eileen! An exquisite bird has just come to my bird feeder! It has a totally black head, or I would think it is a woodpecker. It has black on its back and wings, except for a pure white streak down its back, and some touches of purest white on its wings. It has a snowy-white breast on which there is a scarlet bib, with a little of that brilliant red trailing on down its white breast. It is breathtaking in its beauty!"* Eileen kept leafing through her bird book while I was talking. *"Here it is!"* she exclaimed. *"It's a*

54

rose-breasted grosbeak. It fits your description so perfectly. Does it have a white beak?" "Yes it does — off-white."

I had no sooner hung up the phone, when a pair of indigo buntings appeared at my feeder, followed by a bright red cardinal! *Oh, Father! Oh, dear Father! Surely You sent all these to remind me that Your eye is on more than sparrows, and I can <u>know</u> that You are watching me!*

> Why should I feel discouraged?
> Why should the shadows come?
> Why should my heart be lonely,
> And long for heav'n and home?
> When Jesus is my portion!
> My constant Friend is He,
> His eye is on the sparrow,
> And I *know* He watches me!
>
> Mrs. C. D. Martin

I marvel when I realize that You are watching over all my difficult anniversaries, so lovingly. " . . . <u>*the time*</u> for the singing of birds *is come*." Perhaps the time for me to sing has come, too!

55

No Stars!

". . . neither sun nor stars appeared for many days . . ."
ACTS 27:20

W hat an apt description of grieving this verse is! At the onset of grief the dark sky is unbroken and has not so much as a glimmer of light. There are *no stars* in our sky.

I was recently in Swaziland — so very far south in Africa. I was thrilled to see a star-studded sky like we never see in the Northern Hemisphere. There were so many that I stared incredulously at them and worshiped the God Who made them all. My worship was a spontaneous act!

What a contrast to the sky described here! In this passage describing the starless sky, Paul goes on to tell us, " . . . the storm continued raging, we finally gave up all hope." No way! Even without the stars, I shall not give up hope. It is here the analogy ends, for in the middle of my starless night, there is still the gentle whisper that comes to my spirit, assuring me that He is with me, even to the end of the age. I know that He will see me through this darkest of nights into which not even a firefly dares to flicker.

The wise men kept going even when the star they had seen in the East disappeared. Relentlessly they plodded on in the right direction until the star reappeared, bringing them a new and vibrant joy. All wise men and women do that. When the stars disappear temporarily, they just keep right on plodding. That's what I am doing right now.

No stars? For many days? That's my current lot, but it is temporary, I know that. Faith tells me so. I shall weather this storm, as Paul weathered his, and one day those stars will shine again and shine ever so brightly.

There will be plenty of them, too, like in the Southern Hemisphere. It is there, in that Southern Hemisphere that the cross appears. I have lived all my life in the Northern Hemisphere and for decades had never seen the Southern Cross, but in recent days I have rejoiced to see it. So shall it be in my starless night of grief. The stars will reappear, and in the midst of them the cross shall shine brightly — *the signature of Jesus!*

YOUR DAYS OF MOURNING

" . . . your days of mourning . . . will end."
ISAIAH 60:20B

There is a lot of comfort in this portion of a verse that a special friend sent to me. I do not want to mourn forever. I will love my honey forever — I know that. But I do not want the rest of my life to be characterized by a pain in my heart that will not subside. So, I am comforted by these reassuring words: ". . . your days of mourning . . . *will* end."

My friend, Don Trouten, said to me, "I would not exchange a lesser grief for a lesser love." Nor would I. I realize the pain has been severe, persistent and prolonged. But that pain is born of a depth of love that was very precious to me, and not of a desire to cling to the morbid or to wallow in self-pity.

I have not withdrawn from people, even when I felt like it, with the exception of the pre-planned time for intense grieving right after the funeral. Then I wanted to be alone, and it was right. Now sometimes I want to be alone when it is not right, and I am careful to attempt to know which is which.

On one occasion the Lord Jesus deliberately withdrew from the crowds to be alone. There were other times when I feel certain it would have been a comfortable thing for Him to do, but He deliberately stayed with them. He knew which was the right thing to do, and He knows in my situation, too. I must trust Him for direction, as long as this mourning continues.

Mourning is such a complex activity. It is so personal. It is so lonely at times. It is all consuming. It is so permeating. It can even be devastating. But there is another side to the act of mourning: It can be helpful. It can be therapeutic. It can relieve the spirit and the soul. It can facilitate final closure.

In this verse, my Father tells me that there *will* be a day of closure when *the days of my mourning* will end. Thank you, Lord. I have needed that reassurance, for at times it is difficult to imagine myself feeling any differently all the rest of my days. That's not the truth. Your statement about *the days of mourning* makes that very clear. I am grateful for this clear prediction which I take as a promise.

WHY IS THE SKY BLUE?

"Now I know in part; then I shall know fully . . ."
I CORINTHIANS 13:12B

S ometimes I long to know fully the reasons God decided to take my loved one home. I bow to the sovereignty of God humming, "Sometime I'll understand," but I weep, even while I hum.

An illustration from a book by Garry Hanvey deftly puts all my questions in perspective. He tells about the time his little boy asked him, "Daddy, why is the sky blue?" Garry wrote,

> Now I'm not the greatest father, but when a child of mine asks a question, I want to have an answer for him. So I thought for a minute, "How can I explain this to a three-year-old so he can understand it?"
>
> You see, Justin, the earth (that's this dirt and rock stuff we walk on) is a great big sphere (you know, a ball) hanging in space (well, that's the big, black empty area you see at night), and this big sphere we call earth is rotating — um, going 'round and

'round another gigantic ball of fire called the sun (see it up there?). Well, when the light rays (those are things that light is made of, do you follow me?) from the sun travel through the earth's atmosphere (that's a whole bunch of invisible gases. Gases? — air the stuff we breathe — these light rays are refracted (bent, changed — just stay with me), and the only part of the spectrum (forget it!), the only color that hits our eyes is the color blue. Now, do you understand?

It's not so much that the questions I ask are stupid ones; it's just that those questions are unanswerable at this time because of my inability to comprehend what God would like to tell me.

(Garry continues:)
Here's the answer I gave my son: "It's blue because God made it that way. It must be His favorite color, besides green. What's your favorite color, Justin?"

I know Garry is right. My question has a distinct parallel to a three-year-old asking, *Why is the sky blue?* God cannot fully explain to me why He has taken my sweetheart now. I must wait until I am older and more mature to learn the fullness of His perfect plan. For now, it's just because He wanted her with Him! *

VALLEY OF THE SHADOW

"Even though I walk through the <u>valley of the shadow</u> of death,
I will fear no evil for you are with me."
PSALM 23:41

S hadows have a most unusual quality — they are both
real and unreal. I can step on mine without hurting
myself. It has my form and fleeting likeness, but it lacks
substance.

I don't like this <u>valley of the shadow</u> of death. But then, God
never asked me to like it! He only said that I would not have
to fear evil in the midst of its darkness, nor would I have to
walk here alone. He promised to be with me — and He is!

This terrible separation from someone so dear to me is a
painful one. The deep wound of my grief is continually with
me. It will not go away — not yet. It is a very real and a very
painful experience.

Yet at the same time there is something very *unreal* and
shadowy about this thing called death. My sweetheart is not
dead! She is more vibrantly alive than she ever was when we
enjoyed life together. The quality of life she now enjoys

cannot be compared to the quality of life she had during her illness, nor even prior to that.

People who live in sin are dead while they live. But we who know Christ are alive when we are dead! Oh death, where is your sting? Oh grave, where is your victory? (I Cor. 15:55) You, death, do not have the final say! Your moment of truth is such a fleeting moment. I shall soon be reunited with my sweetheart in the most joyful reunion we have *ever* had (and we had some very precious ones that are happy memories).

It takes sunshine to make a shadow. Thank You, Lord, for the sunshine of Your love that is never totally eclipsed. Thank You for helping me to keep things in perspective while I am walking through this dreadful *Valley of the Shadow*. I can deliberately remind my mangled heart through my persistent tears that I do not have to fear evil. *You*, my gentle, faithful, loving Shepherd *are with me* all the remaining days of my life.   *

You will Rejoice

"Now is your time of grief, but I will see you again and you will rejoice, and no one will take away your joy."
JOHN 16:22

I am aware that I am lifting a truth out of its context here and making a new application of it, but in a way that's what Jesus was doing, too. He was using an analogy. So am I.

This is my time of grief, but I know I am going to see my sweetheart again and that brings rejoicing to my heart. It is a joy that no one can take from me.

We lived all our Christian lives knowing that, because we had eternal life, there was nothing that could permanently separate us — not even death! Now I must apply that truth to my current situation. I want to do it so thoroughly that no one and nothing can take away my joy.

Now is your time of grief. Hearing those words come from the mouth of the Lord Jesus helps me to accept this, my time of grief. It is almost as if He is saying that this grief was specifically assigned to me as a part of the totality of my earth experience.

Someday I will understand how that every last thing that happened to me was a part of the intricate and beautiful plan the Lord had laid out. Even my honey's very difficult days were a part of God's permissive will for her. I cannot fully understand that, nor will I try. I will just accept the fact that this is *my time of grief* and by God's grace I am to make the very most of it. I am to remember that I *can* rejoice, even in the midst of such heartache. And *no one can take away my joy*, not even the enemy of my soul (though he would love to).

I will see you again. When Jesus says that to me, I thrill. When I say it about my sweetheart, I thrill. Heaven is certainly more precious to me than it used to be, even though I had others I was looking forward to seeing there. There is no one dearer to me than the darling of my heart — other than Jesus Himself!   *

WHAT IS THERE TO LIVE FOR?

"It's in Christ that we find out who we are and <u>what we are living for</u>.
Long before we heard of Christ . . . he had his eye on us, had designs on us
for glorious living . . ."
EPHESIANS 1:11, 12 THE MESSAGE

Who am I now, and <u>what do I have to live for?</u> Actually, I am still the same person I was in God's sight, though in the sight of man I am someone else. To them I am a widower, a person to feel sorry for at appropriate times, a "single." I have not grown accustomed to any of those new categories yet. Sometimes I really feel at loose ends. But how I feel does not really affect who I am.

Previously God had things He was working in my life through my honey. Now He has things He wants to work in my life quite apart from my honey.

I am a Christian — that's who I am! I am a son of God and a joint-heir with Jesus Christ, His Son — that's who I am! I am a servant who can still do useful things for my Master, Who still has work for me to do — that's who I am!

Yes, I have very significant things yet to do for my Lord. I am still living here, while the one so dear to me has been taken away, only because He still has work for me to do.

I must never miss hearing the assignments He gives me. It would be possible for me to become so insulated by my own grief that He could not easily get through to me. When He fixed His eye upon me, and chose to bring my sweetheart into my life, His plans did not extend only to the length of her life. They went beyond that. How far beyond only time will tell. *Glorious living* is beyond my ability to comprehend just now when I am hurting as I am. But it is still a part of what He has in mind for me. I must never forget that.

So, I must look to Christ Himself to *find out who I am and what I have to live for.* What I find there will be not only satisfying, but also rewarding and even exciting, so as to fulfill His promise of *glorious living.* His *designs on me* are exhilarating!*

DARKNESS AND SHADOWS

"He reveals the deep things of darkness and brings deep
shadows into the light."
JOB 12:22

There are words in this verse that are very descriptive of
the days following my sweetheart's homegoing.
Darkness and shadows accurately depict the way many of my
days could be characterized. She was a major source of my
"sunshine" and she was taken away. But she was not the *only*
source of my sunshine. I thank the Lord for that. Jesus, Who
is the Light, has also been a major part of my sunshine, and
He is still with me.

I must keep the "You are my sunshine!" and the "sunlight,
sunlight all along the way" parts of my life ever clearly before
me. Then, although the sunlight my honey provided is gone,
the Sunlight that comes from the Son's light will still be
lighting my way. I need that Sonlight right now. I deliberately
draw upon it. I realize I have my small part in it, just as I have
my small part in lighting a dark room at night, when I throw
the switch as I enter the room. Instantly there is light. The
darkness is dispelled. I can see clearly because of a switch,

and wires and light bulbs, and a distant power plant and the payment of last month's bill.

My small part is to flick the switch to another position. Lord, teach me where the switches are that will bring instant light into the darkened rooms of my heart. I want *the deep things of darkness* to be revealed and the *deep shadows* to be dispelled by the light.

I realize that You are speaking here about *darkness and shadows* that are really significant, for You use the word "deep" in connection with them both.

Depths never troubled You. They must not overwhelm me. And they will not, as long as I remember not only Who You are, but also what You have promised to do. Oh, "Shine, Jesus, shine" into this dark valley in a way that will make the pathway very clear and will reveal to me the things that need to be revealed so that I will not stumble, and so that I will be Divinely comforted.

THERE'S A SONG IN MY HEART

"You shall have a song ..."
ISAIAH 30:29A

A letter came today from my good friend, Charles
Young. He recently lost his precious wife to cancer. He
told me that he has actually sung a solo in church! I loved his
account of it, "Before I sang I dedicated the piece to all who
had supported us during our trial. Then I said, 'Many of you
have asked me how I am doing. This song will tell you how I
am doing, and also *how I am doing it*.' Then I sang ... I'll send
you a tape. The words express how God is always with us in
all His fatherly caring ways. When I finished there were few
dry eyes. Many thanked and hugged me in support."

I've answered him already. I said I wondered what it was
he sang. I told him I knew what I would sing. It is a very
special song to me — one that I feel as though God has
given. I have memorized it:

Day by day and with each passing moment,
Strength I find to meet my trials here.

70

Trusting in my Father's wise bestowment,
    I've no cause for worry or for fear.
He Whose heart is kind beyond all measure
    Gives unto each day what He deems best;
Lovingly its part of pain or pleasure,
    Mingling toil with peace and rest.
Help me then, in every tribulation
    So to trust Your promises, O Lord,
That I lose not faith's sweet consolation
    Offered me within Your Holy Word.
Help me, Lord, when grief and trouble meeting,
    Just to take, as from my Father's hand,
One by one, the days, the moments fleeting
    'Till I reach the promised land.

A. L. Skoog

I looked forward to receiving his tape to know what *his* choice was. Then it happened! When preparing this devotional for my heart (and yours), I was checking my quote from his letter in my obsession for accuracy, and I saw the words I had missed because of my poor habit of scanning while reading, instead of reading every word. He had actually written, "Then I sang 'Day by Day'. . ."

So, our choices were identical! *The song God put in his heart* was the same one the Lord has put in mine!   *

I GRIEVE FOR YOU

"I grieve for you . . . you were very dear to me. Your love for
me was wonderful . . ."
II SAMUEL 1:26

These words of David make me feel all the closer to him. His psalms have been such a consistent comfort throughout our ordeal. Here I find him saying the same kinds of things I say about my sweetheart, and *to* my sweetheart.

He is talking about (and to) his dear friend. My honey was my dear friend — my *dearest* friend!

I am intrigued by the fact that David is talking to his friend *who is dead!* I talk to my sweetheart, too, at times. I do it when I am alone, of course, and no one can hear me. I wonder what people would think? On the other hand, what difference does it make what they would think? If David, "a man after God's own heart" could do it, and even have it recorded for all the world to "hear" him, then I don't have to worry about talking out loud to my honey when I am alone. Sometimes aloneness is not all that bad. There is a special privacy it affords. There is a special privilege it grants. In the seclusion of my empty house I can speak aloud to the darling of my heart and not worry about whether people conclude that I am losing my mind!

That's precisely what I do. I say the very words David said, "*I grieve for you . . . you were very dear to me. Your love for me was wonderful.*" I tell her how much I miss her. I tell her how much those years He gave us together meant to me. I tell her I look forward to the wonderful day when I shall be able to hold her in my arms again. I tell her I want to be with her for all eternity, and then I take comfort in knowing that *I shall!*

Why should I not grieve for her? Why should I not remember how dear she was to me and how wonderful her love was? I doubt there is anyone who can give me a good reason, other than some misguided psychologist who does not speak from experience! Thank you, David, for paving the way by all you said about — and to — your dear friend, Jonathan.   *

A CORD OF THREE STRANDS

"A cord of three strands is not quickly broken."
ECCLESIASTES 4:12

There is an aspect of being without my honey that I do not like at all. It is the awkwardness that I feel when I am with almost any couple. Suddenly we are three, and there is something "uneven" about three, or five, or seven. But those numbers have abruptly thrust themselves into my life uninvited.

I remember all the times when my sweetheart and I worked so hard at getting my widowed sister-in-law to know that we really wanted her to be with us. We felt we understood her reluctance and we diligently strove to break it down. I am so glad we did. Very few friends work that hard at breaking down *my* reluctance.

I didn't fully understand her feelings. I couldn't. But now I do. At banquets I look for the table that has one seat left, so I won't take the place some couple could have. I choose the end seat at a long table so the couples can take places together along the sides. But — it is painful for me to

74

rehearse all this; I must stop it and deliberately think in a positive vein.

Three is not an unpleasant number with God. He enjoys the relationships within the Trinity. Why did He choose to exist in *three* Persons? Why not four? Is it because He is not at all uncomfortable with a threesome, the way I am? He experiences none of the things that stigmatize the number three in our culture. We say, "Two's company; three's a crowd." God says that, "*a cord of three strands is not quickly broken.*" He sees the strength in triple things. I will too! With God's help, I will.

I will accept invitations that generate a threesome. I will refuse to worry about what my presence does to the "balance." I will bring His grace into every locale where my presence causes the number to be uneven. I will so live in His presence that people will be glad I sat at their table or accepted their invitation. I will take Jesus with me wherever I go, and if people are uncomfortable about our human trinity, then we will together metamorphose into a fabulous foursome!

HURT, BUT NOT DESTROYED

"We are . . . troubled but not crushed; sometimes in doubt, but never in despair; there are many enemies, but we are never without a friend; and though badly <u>hurt</u> at times, we are <u>not destroyed</u>."
II CORINTHIANS 4:8, 9 TODAY'S ENGLISH VERSION

Paul, you have described me to a "T." You do not ignore my troubled, doubt-ridden, paranoid, pain-filled condition, but you show me the other side of those coins. The "change" in my pocket is mangled. The scarred, discolored coins that I like to get rid of quickly seem to predominate. Yet the truth is that a quarter is a quarter, even when someone has disfigured it badly. A penny is still a penny, even when it has lost all its bright copper luster. A dime is still a dime when the Statue of Liberty is barely discernible.

No, I have no mint-condition collectors' items to hold in my hand for others to admire, but I am far from bankrupt! Each coin still has its value — the same value it always had. Perhaps it is even worth more! I have realized that though I am troubled, my enemy has not been allowed to crush me. I do doubt some of the hopes for the future that I held onto strongly before, but I do not despair nor feel hopeless. In the midst of such formidable enemies as Death himself and the cold grave, I have found that my Friend Who stays closer than a brother is there to put his loving arms around me. My honey was not the only one to go into the arms of Jesus!

Yes, I will admit that I am badly _hurt, but_ I also know that I have _not_ been _destroyed_, and I shall not be! My enemy is not strong enough to do that, for greater is He that is in me than he that is in the world. He can bring tears and pain and heartache and death _only_ when God permits him to.

To deny my troubled heart, my doubts, my loneliness and my pain would be both foolish and unhealthful. I don't have to do that to be spiritual! What I do need to do is to remind my heart that I am not crushed. I am not in despair. I am not friendless. _I am not destroyed_ — nor shall I be! My loving Savior is right here with me to assure me of all these perks.   *

THE BEST PATHWAY FOR YOUR LIFE

"You are my hiding place from every storm of life . . . I will instruct you
(says the Lord) and guide you along <u>the best pathway for your life</u>; I will
advise you and watch your progress."
PSALM 32:7, 8   THE LIVING BIBLE

P eople often tell me I should not make my decisions too
quickly just now. I know they are right. Yet some
decisions have to be made, and I don't know what is best. I
have already made one incorrect decision.

I need to depend on You, Lord, for the wisdom to make
right decisions. How comforting to come across this
wonderful promise that You will *guide me along <u>the best pathway</u>*
<u>for my life</u>. That's so definite, and it is explicitly what I am
needing. I thrill to read this promise and must remember it
when I feel concerned about the decisions I need to make.

When my sweetheart was living, You guided the two of us
beautifully, time and time again. I must remember that Your
very nature is to guide those who look to You for direction.
You will surely do no less for me now when I feel the need of
Your guidance more than I ever have.

78

My dear helpmate was the person who wisely evaluated my decision-making. Now I am alone. I really need to listen for the gentle whisper that will say to me, "This is the way, walk in it" (Isa. 30:21). Or, perhaps that voice will just say, "No!" when I am headed in the wrong direction. You can give me a deep settled sense of peace when I am headed in the right one.

The best pathway for my life — I like that phrase. I find comfort in that reassurance. I marvel at the follow-up, too, for You promise not only to *advise m*e but also to *monitor my progress*! What loving and fatherly attentiveness from One Who is all-wise, and Who has never made a wrong decision!

Yes, some are saying this is a dangerous time for me, when I could so easily make the wrong decisions. I do appreciate their concern, but I am comforted to know that wrong decisions are not really anything I have to worry too much about — *if I am listening!* *

SUMMER AND WINTER

"You made both summer and winter."
PSALM 74:17

How different summertime is from wintertime! During the one I resort to air-conditioning to remain comfortable. During the other I pay high fuel bills for the same purpose. During the one I delight to watch things grow and during the other I wait for them to start growing again. There are numerous contrasts.

In life there are *summertimes and wintertimes*, too. I am currently enduring my most severe "winters." So are some of my friends. I must be faithful in asking God to help them through their bitterly cold winters.

As severe as my own winter is currently, I recognize that there are those who have a storm worse than mine to weather. At least I have been able to remain above depression, with a special enabling the Lord Himself has given. That in itself is not a small gift!

Looking back, I remember with joy the "summertimes" the Lord gave us repeatedly during our lifetime together. While I cannot enjoy this "wintertime," I can keep warm by reminding my heart of His loving faithfulness to us in the past and by immersing myself in the wonderful promises He has made to me. I must never forget that my God is in complete control. "He knows the way that I take and when I am come forth I shall be as gold," Job could say in the midst of his long winter. The gold he refers to will be gold that is pure and precious and valued by the Lord, having been refined by the fire. Gold that has endured both *summer and winter*.

> *Summer and winter* and springtime and harvest,
> Sun, moon and stars in their courses above,
> Join with all nature in manifold witness
> To Thy great faithfulness, mercy and love.
>
> T. O. Chisholm

Yes, great is Thy faithfulness, Master of both *summer and winter*. Help me to accept my wintertime, confident that another summer is coming. This is no *perma*frost. The flowers of spring will surely bloom once again — *then comes summer!* *

A STRENGTHENED FRAME

"The LORD will . . . satisfy your needs in a sun-scorched land and will
strengthen your frame."
ISAIAH 58:11

The Bible is filled with wonderful promises. Those promises are in an entirely different category from the promises I hear the politicians make. God's promises are sure and trustworthy. They are backed by an integrity our world knows little about. He keeps each promise with ease. He has made none of them thoughtlessly.

The satisfying of my *needs in a sun-scorched land* has a lot of appeal to me right now. The heat was intense in the trial through which my sweetheart and I have passed. It robbed us of so much that had shaded and beautified our lives earlier. I really need divine help in the satisfying of my needs in this *sun-scorched* terrain. The *strengthening of my frame* is a specific need also. Both are promised here. I must actively appropriate these promises, and receive the refreshing He has pledged.

Standing on the promises of Christ, my King,

Through eternal ages let His praises ring,
"Glory in the highest!" I will shout and sing,
Standing on the promises of God.

Standing on the promises that cannot fail
When the howling storms of doubt and fear assail,
By the living word of God I shall prevail,
Standing on the promises of God.

Standing on the promises, I cannot fall,
Listening every moment to the Spirit's call,
Resting in my Savior as my all in all,
Standing on the promises of God.

R. Kelso Carter

This verse gives me two of the thousands of promises on which I may stand. *The Lord will . . . satisfy your needs in a sun-scorched land* and *the Lord will . . . strengthen your frame.* I need them both and I will claim the fulfillment of them.

IF WE DIDN'T HAVE THE LORD

"If we didn't have the LORD," Israel should say, "If we didn't have the LORD . . ."
PSALM 124:1, 2

Ah, but I do! My heart rejoices when I stop to think of the difference it makes to have a loving Lord who is touched by my feelings.

If I didn't have the Lord, how different things would be! I cannot imagine how those who do not have the Lord get through this dark valley. I lean on Him heavily. I hold fast to His hand when I cannot see. I turn to Him for fellowship when I am lonely. I put my trust in Him when I am afraid. I turn my face heavenward sometimes when I weep. And always there is the beautiful reassurance that He really cares about my grieving, my loneliness, my pain. I recall a gospel song we sang often when I was a child:

> One is walking with me over life's uneven way,
>> Constantly supporting me each moment of the day;

84

How can I be lonely when such fellowship is mine,
  With my blessed Lord divine?

Days may bring their burdens and their trials as I go,
  But my Lord is near and helps to make them lighter
  grow.
Life may have its crosses, or its losses or increase,
  Jesus meets them all with peace.

In the hour of *sad bereavement* or of *bitter loss.*
  I can find support and consolation at the cross;
Want or woe or suffering all seem glorified when He
  Daily walks and talks with me.

Chorus

How can I be lonely when I've Jesus only
  To be my companion and unfailing guide?
Why should I be weary, or my path seem dreary,
  When He's walking by my side.

Haldor Lillenas

If I didn't have the Lord . . . Oh, how thankful I am that I do,
and that the gospel song accurately reflects the way He
comforts "in the hour of sad bereavement or of bitter loss."

Haldor Lillenas also wrote, "It is glory just to walk with
Him." Yes, it is! I do have the Lord. That makes a great deal
of difference in how I handle my shadowed pathway, my
crosses and my losses.

If I didn't have the Lord . . . But, I do!

HE WILL SURELY BE GRACIOUS

That certainly is reassuring! He hears my cry (and my crying) and He is gracious to me in response.

I go alone sometimes to grieve — at a friend's cottage, or even just into the bathroom so I can wash my eyes with cold water when I finish crying, in the hopes that no one will know I have just had a good cry. But my Heavenly Father sees me crying, hears me, and embraces me tenderly. Yes, "Jesus knows, and best of all He cares, and I belong to Him."

Both points of this verse of Scripture indicate pointedly that we should cry aloud. I do that. When I am alone in my house, or in the car, where I am sure no one can hear me, there are times when I cry right out loud. Lord, help me the next time I do that to remember this verse. Help me to remember that You are not only hearing those cries, but also that You are reaching out toward me with arms of love.

I remember the time, Lord Jesus, when I was driving to Asheville and began crying so hard I nearly had to stop the car. I cried out aloud, "Lord Jesus, please help me! I need You to heal my broken heart. I am so horribly wounded. I am grieving so deeply!" And You did! From the moment that audible anguished heartcry escaped my lips, there came a distinct and noticeable lessening of the pain. It is a moment I will not forget.

You were fulfilling the promise of this very verse and I had not yet read this promise. That tells me there are promises You have made that You keep even if we are not aware You have made them!

Yes, some things are as sure as the Rock of Gibraltar, and this is one of them — that You will hear my cries and will respond to them lovingly and graciously. So then, let me not shrink from crying aloud, then.

You will surely be gracious to me at the sound of my cry. When you hear it, You will answer me. I find a lot of comfort in this practical, earthy promise.

YOU WILL NOT ABANDON ME

"Because of your great compassion you did not abandon them in the desert."
NEHEMIAH 9:19A

L ord, I too am in a desert. In some ways it is the driest desert I have ever encountered. I am very confident that You do not plan to abandon me here. You have not changed. You are the same today as You were yesterday, and You will be the same forever.

The desert is not a pleasant place. I look forward to the day when You will bring me out of it and I shall again enjoy verdant, growing, living things, as well as refreshing, cool streams.

For the present my lot is to plod through the hot sand of loneliness, heartache, melancholy and sometime listlessness brought on by the "heat." The heat is enervating. The sand burns my toes. Yet, *even here* I shall praise you. The song I sang with gusto when things were going well is still a comfort now that my world has caved in: "Whatever my lot, Thou hast taught me to say, 'It is well, it is well with my soul!' " The promise that meant so much to me then sustains my soul now: "I will be with you always, even to the very end . . . "

Help me never to give serious attention to the questions Satan tries to establish in my mind. Let me take refuge in the wonderful truth that

Christ is the answer to my every need.
  Christ is the answer, He is my Friend indeed.
Problems of life my spirit may assail;
  With Christ as Savior, I shall never fail —
For, Christ is the answer to my need!

Unknown

All I have need of is found in a Person, You! My heartache results from the loss of a very special person. No one on earth was ever dearer to me, except you, dear Lord Jesus! You are still here with me — *You will never abandon me.* Certainly not in this brutal wilderness!

No, the desert does not have much in it that appeals to me. I much prefer a rain forest. But You, Who made the lush rain forest, also made the barren wastelands, and You are omnipresent.

No matter how long it takes me to traverse this emotional Sahara, *You will be with me.* Of that I am certain!   *

CONTINUAL SURVEILLANCE

*"From heaven the LORD looks down and sees all mankind; from His
dwelling place He watches all who live on earth — He who forms the
hearts of all, who considers everything they do."*
PSALM 33:13-15

This is a *powerful* truth. Unfortunately it has been used to
threaten God's people with the emphasis being placed
on God's seeing every *evil* deed of man. Though that *is* the
truth, and it certainly is a deterrent from evil, it is much more
encouraging to apply this truth to my needs and the happy
recognition that I am continually observed and protected by
my loving Lord. He watches over me and He considers
everything I do. David expressed it so forcefully in the 139th
Psalm:

> "O Lord, you have searched me and you know me.
> You know when I sit down and when I rise . . . You
> discern my going out and my lying down; you are
> familiar with all my ways. Before a word is on my
> tongue, you know it completely . . . When I was
> woven together . . . your eyes saw my unformed

body. All the days ordained for me were written in your book before one of them came to be . . . how precious . . ."

Such omniscience is both staggering to my mind *and* comforting to my spirit. Nothing ever escapes the notice of God. He knows my every need and in His great love He comes to my rescue. Based upon previous experience, it is not unrealistic for me to expect great and mighty things from my loving, all-powerful God.

In my bad moments as well as in my good ones, but especially when my grief surfaces with great force, I need to remember the encouraging truths set forth in these three verses. I need to remind myself that God has not lost control, and He never will.

From heaven the LORD *looks down and sees all mankind; from His dwelling place He watches all who dwell on earth — He who forms the hearts of all, who considers everything they do.*

In His Time!

"Woe to those who say, 'Let God hurry, let him hasten his work . . . ' "
Isaiah 5:18, 19

At times I long for You to work more quickly, Lord. I want a healing of memories. I want the pain in my chest to go away. I want relief from my tears that flow so often. It is easy for me to pray, please *hasten Your work in me!*

This passage makes me stop and think. You know the desires of my heart. There is no way I can hide them from You. I do want to be submissive to your way of working. I know You always do what is best and in my best interest. I really do know that.

I am impatient by nature. When that driver ahead of me waited and waited, refusing to pull out onto the highway, I found myself saying aloud, "There! That's an opening big enough — go for it!" He neither heard me nor saw it as I saw it. I became increasingly frustrated over wasting those minutes. That's how I am. I need to get on with life, no matter what the situation is. I don't like that disquieting part of my nature. I need Your help to change it.

I want to be able to say, and mean it, "Take Your time, dear Father, take Your time. You know how a wound should heal, and that permitting it to close over too soon would not be best for me."

Shall I question "The Great Physician" when I know so little about grief myself? I am a novice in this matter — You are not. Just take Your time and meanwhile help me to be patient.

I love that little chorus, "*In His time, in His time.* God makes everything beautiful *in His time.* My heart responds by singing, "*In Your time, in Your time*, please make all things beautiful, *in Your time.*"

Already You have done wonderful things for me. I have not slipped into a clinical depression, though my loss (which is fundamental to all depression) was the greatest of my entire life. I have been able to begin to enjoy life again, with an appreciation for beauty, and enjoyment of music and an occasional delight in being with others. You are working, in a timely manner. *In Your time*, dear Lord Jesus, *in Your time.* *

COMFORT FOR THE MISERABLE

". . . God . . . comforts those who feel miserable . . ."
II CORINTHIANS 7:6 BECK

Only to my friends — my dearest friends — do I admit that sometimes *I feel miserable*. Most of the time I wear my mask pretty well, I think. It is not everybody's business that I am laughing on the outside and crying on the inside.

With my closest friends I can remove this stuffy, suffocating mask and let the tears flow. Yet, even with them I feel myself struggling with those tears, when I do that. Why? It is only when I am alone with my Best Friend that I allow the tears and even the out-loud sobbings find expression. In those rare honest moments, the loving Lord, Who *comforts those who feel miserable*, comforts me. How I praise Him!

There is not a single one of my *miserable* moments when He does not see behind my "Fine, thank you," traditional response to greetings. He reacts with an outpouring of comfort. "Man looks on the outward appearance, but my loving God looks upon (my) heart." There is nothing hidden from Him.

94

"Jesus knows, and best of all He cares, and I belong to Him." Every part of me belongs to Him — my life, my body, my mind, my emotions. Even my intangibles are fully known to Him and belong to Him. By "intangibles" I mean my shattered dreams, my grief, my uncertainties, my struggles, my anguish, my "half-ness." All of those things are fully known to Him and He is my God who _comforts those who feel miserable_.

Oh, I don't feel that way all the time. Such grieving would do me in — literally! But I do have my moments, and it is a great source of comfort to me to read here in Beck's translation, as well as in the Jerusalem Bible that He is a loving God who _comforts those who feel miserable_.

I respond with an intense love for You, my loving Lord, and I thank You for caring about my _miserable_ condition — caring so deeply!   *

UNTIL THIS STORM IS PAST

"O God, have pity, for I am trusting you! I will hide beneath the shadow of your wings until this storm is past. I will cry to the God of heaven who does such wonderful things for me, because of his love and his faithfulness."
PSALM 57:1-3

This is a storm, Father! The sun is obliterated. The rains come. The chill blasts buffet me. I shrink from the discomfort and cower when the lightning strikes too close to me. My emotions are raw and unpredictable. The songwriter insisted, "The Lord's our Rock, in Him we hide, a shelter in the time of storm" (V. J. Charlesworth). Yes, You are a shelter to me, dear Lord.

"The shadow of Your wings," "His love," "His faithfulness" are all mentioned in this passage as things that make the storm more tolerable. I don't know what I should do without them. I am no super-human Christian who rises above all my personal agony in glorious spiritual victory, and acts as if I have learned how to "count it all joy." In fact some days my "joy" account seems totally depleted, even overdrawn! I loved my spouse with my whole heart, and I am only being honest

when I say that the pain of this separation is the most acute I have ever endured.

What a comfort it is to hide behind the protective shadow of Your wings *until this terrible storm is past*. I find great security there, my Father. Your love and Your faithfulness are a wonderful consolation to me. I draw long draughts from the flask of *faithfulness* and crawl beneath Your down-filled comforter. There, in a fetal position before You, my curled-up spirit does not shrivel up. It is warmed and blessed and reminded that Your *faithfulness* is great and Your *love* is everlasting.

You know the way that I, too, take and when I am come out of this I shall be as gold. Job was certain of that (Job 23:10). I am also. *This storm will pass* and I shall once again stand erect and ready to face my world, by the grace of my faithful, comforting Lord. Until it does, "*I will hide beneath the shadow of Your wings.*"

A RESCUE OPERATION

". . . you and your prayers are a part of <u>the rescue operation</u> . . . I can see your faces even now, lifted in praise of God's deliverance of (me), a rescue in which your prayers played such a crucial part."
II CORINTHIANS 1:11   THE MESSAGE

T here are times when I feel I need to be delivered from these powerful, painful, persistent emotions. *A rescue operation* is in order. At such times I wonder if my friends really know how much I need their prayers.

Then I ask myself, *How often have I responded to a burden to pray for someone I know who needs a rescue — someone who would call me his friend?* I can think of someone right now. I shall stop to pray . . . and now, having prayed, I recall that God turned things around for Job when he prayed for his friends (Job 42:10)! So then, God has designed His *rescue operation* in such a way that I play a part when I am faithful in praying for others. I know He is faithful in laying me upon the hearts of sensitive, tender, caring Christians. I do not want them to pray for me while I fail to be a part of *a rescue operation* in someone else's life.

The works of God are beautifully and impressively interwoven. He lifts me up as I lift up others in prayer. He forgives me my sins against Him as I forgive others their sins against me (Matt. 6:14). He gives to me when I give to others (Luke 6:38).

There is a remarkable sense in which I become a part of my own _rescue operation_ as I participate in the _rescue operation_ of my friends. My prayers play _a crucial part_; their prayers play _a crucial part_.

There is something about this reciprocal ministry that I like. It is so much like our creative Lord to weave together the fabric of our spiritual lives in this intriguing manner.

Help me to be very faithful in doing my part, dear Lord. I really need to have others be faithful in doing their part. Rescue operations demand swift action. Make me very sensitive to the times when you want me to spring into action for dear friends.   *

THE HIDDEN MEANING

". . . He told us the hidden meaning of his will."
EPHESIANS 1:9   BECK

Will I ever know, while here on earth, the *why* of what has happened? I may — I may not. Sometimes God does tell us *"the hidden meaning of His will."* I love it when He does, but He is not obligated to.

Those times when God has drawn back the veil and permitted me to see His marvelous plan are extra special to me. The other side of the coin is that there are times when I can make no sense at all out of the way God is working. Even in those times, I am thankful that deep in my heart there is a strong consciousness that my loving Father does all things well. I know that someday I will surely know the hidden meaning.

Not now, but in the coming years,
　　It may be in the better land,
I'll read the meaning of my tears,
　　And there, sometime I'll understand.

100

I'll catch the broken thread again;
  And finish what I here began;
Heaven will the mysteries explain,
  And then, ah then, I'll understand.

I'll know why clouds instead of sun
  Were over many a cherished plan;
Why song has ceased when scarce begun;
  'Tis there, sometime, I'll understand.

I think the theology of that poetry is quite sound, for God has told us that we shall know as we are known. Our understanding will be profound in that day, when the eyes of our understanding are enlightened. He plans to reveal to us the mysteries of His grace, and I think included among those mysteries for me will be the why of my sweetheart's early homegoing.

Then trust in God through all thy days,
  Fear not, for He doth hold thy hand;
Though dark thy way, still sing and praise,
  Sometime, sometime (you'll) understand.

Maxwell N. Cornelius

I cannot understand now. But I can trust now. That's my current role and I plan to play it well. I will await with eagerness the unfolding of His plan, the revealing of *the hidden meaning of His will.*

VALLEY OF WEEPING

"Happy are those who are strong in the Lord, who want above all else to follow your steps. When they walk through the Valley of Weeping it will become a place of springs where pools of blessing and refreshment collect after rains! They will grow constantly in strength and each of them is invited to meet with the Lord . . ."
PSALM 84:5-7A   THE LIVING BIBLE

What beautiful things are written here about *the Valley of Weeping!* It is not pictured as a dark, forbidding valley from which I instinctively shrink back, and out of which I am desperate to climb.

Blessing, refreshment, strength, and fellowship are all mentioned as profitable adjuncts of tears. That's a perspective I don't readily grasp because it is contrary to my association with tears. Basically I connect tears with sorrow and loss. I only welcome weeping when the tears are tears of joy. That's a very human trait. Even the psalmist associates weeping with the night and joy with the morning when he reminds me that "weeping may remain for a night, but rejoicing comes in the morning" (Psalm 30:5, NIV).

102

I note that the psalmist does call the place of weeping a *valley*, but he insists that it is a profitable valley. He speaks of *"pools of blessing and refreshment"* as well as of *constant growth in strength*. Then comes the apex of all the benefits: an *invitation to meet with the Lord!* The contents of these three verses are almost beyond my grasp. A victory over weeping is depicted here that is so beautiful it seems almost unreal. Actually it *is* unreal, except for the true Christian. A person who is not alive in Christ knows nothing of this kind of victory because of not knowing the Lord Jesus Who has made all of these Valley of Weeping blessings possible.

Happy are those who are strong in the Lord . . . the <u>Valley of Weeping</u> . . . will become a place of springs where pools of blessing and refreshment collect after rains! They will grow constantly in strength and each of them is invited to meet with the Lord . . .

WHEN I WAS IN GREAT NEED

". . . When I was in great need, he saved me."
PSALM 116:6B

What was that great need to which the psalmist was referring. "The cords of death entangled me, the anguish of the grave came upon me; I was overcome by trouble and sorrow" (vs. 3).

I am certain that only those who have gone through what I am going through can fully understand what is meant by *the anguish of the grave*. If the Lord Jesus tarries, almost all of them will know eventually.

The company of those who truly empathize is small. I have no desire that it should be any larger. What I do wish for others is that when the day comes that they are called upon to experience *the anguish of the grave*, they will be able to say along with me that, in response to their anguished cry, "O Lord, save me!" (vs. 4) their compassionate, gracious Lord (vs. 5) did just that.

I dearly love this Psalm! The conclusion to the thoughts in this first part of the Psalm is, "Be at rest once more, O my soul, for the Lord has been good to you. For you, O Lord, have delivered my . . . eyes from tears, my feet from stumbling, that I may walk before the Lord in the land of the living" (vss. 7-9).

I must walk *in the land of the living*. I have to go on living. At first it was difficult, but now new joys are blossoming, bright spots are appearing. My laughter is returning, even if not as hearty as it used to be — that will come. Slowly He is delivering my eyes from tears. One day all tears will be wiped away. Perhaps not here, but assuredly there. I have His promise of that. God Himself plans to wipe those tears from my eyes (Rev. 7:17, 21:4). God can do that even here. There are moments when I feel the warmth of His loving touch, when He sees my tears and responds to them tenderly.

I admit that my need has been great, but I also affirm that *when I was in great need, He saved me.* I can say that with every bit as much conviction as the Psalmist. God is no respecter of persons. He has *saved me* as I have cried out to Him.   *

WHAT KEEPS ME GOING

"It's what we trust in but don't yet see that keeps us going. Do you suppose a few ruts in the road or rocks in the path are going to stop us?"
II CORINTHIANS 5:7, 8 THE MESSAGE

There is no question but that the things I *trust in but do not yet see* are the things *that keep me going*. I will not allow *ruts* or *rocks* to detour me, or stop me. In the divine strength that God Himself provides I will plod on, even if my heart is heavy and I feel a depth of loneliness that only those who have walked this path before me fully understand.

I walk with Him, and though I cannot see the future, I know He controls that future. Though at times I cannot even see which way I should turn in the blanket of darkness that engulfs me, I know that "He knows the way that I take," and I just hold His hand more tightly.

Walking by faith rather than by sight is not totally foreign to me. In earlier days there have been practice sessions for this dark trek. My Lord did not suddenly plunge me into this without preparation. Nor will He abandon me in the midst of this faith walk. Of that I am very confident.

I keep going, sometimes with a very heavy heart, and often with tears, but I do not stop. It would be foolish to. My honey finished her course in spiritual triumph — and so shall I! Spurred on by what I *"trust in but don't yet see," I keep going*.

Ruts and *rocks* were predicted by the Lord Jesus. I heard Him! His words, "In the world you shall have tribulation" did not fall on deaf ears. Nor did the rest of that promise, " . . . but be of good cheer, I have overcome the world" (John 16:33, KJV).

My Overcomer enables me to be an overcomer. I trust in Him, and though I do not see why He has permitted what happened, I do trust, and *that keeps me going*. "Great is Thy faithfulness, O God my Father. There is no shadow of turning with Thee." I want there to be none with *me*, either. *

THE POWERLESS

*"LORD, there is no one like you to help the powerless against
the mighty."*
II CHRONICLES 14:11B

At times I feel like I am among *the powerless* as I come
against the mighty surges of grief that sweep over me
unexpected, unannounced, unwelcomed. What is this thing
called "grief"? How can it have such sudden powers, enabling
it to play with my emotions as if they were toys to be picked
up at will and tossed helter-skelter, shattering my stability?

It invades my happy conversations and pleasant times with
a startling suddenness. For example, when it was time to sit
down at her lovely table with a view of the woods, Gloria said
to Elaine Hopkins and me, "Charles and Elaine can sit there
where the views are best." I hope she didn't sense how close
the tears came to the surface in a rush that nearly bowled me
over — my sweetheart's name was Elaine, too! Until May 19th
of last year it was <u>always</u>, "Charles and Elaine."

Now my joys have been halved and my pain has been
doubled, whereas for forty years my troubles were halved and
my joys doubled. That could amount to a distressing

mathematical compounding, with my joys becoming one-fourth what they used to be and my heartaches becoming three times what they were. But my loving Lord deliberately works on that mathematical formula for me, throwing in a divine equation.

I may feel *powerless,* but only as long as I am looking at my own strength. When I look at His, I flex my muscles and boast, "I can do all things through Christ, Who strengthens me." And that is not whistling in the dark! It is a fact — a glorious fact! Grief may launch many a surprise attack, attempting to blindside me, but I can still be victorious.

I had victory as we sat down at that table. I fought back the tears, and I don't think any of the other three knew the skirmish that took place at that moment. They didn't need to know. The battle wasn't even mine, but the Lord's. The Mighty One helped *the powerless* once again, just as He has promised:

Lord, there is no one like You to help the powerless . . .

A SURE FOUNDATION

"He will be the sure foundation for your times . . . the fear of the LORD
is the key to this treasure."
ISAIAH 33:6

My foot could so easily slip on this difficult path the
Lord has included in my earthly experience except
that He Himself provides a sure footing. I have never walked
this way before, and I find all kinds of new and treacherous
aspects to this footpath. But, though I have never traversed
this path before, *He has!*

Job articulated this truth so succinctly when he said, "He
knows the way that I take . . ." That very comforting
statement was made by one whose path was rougher than
mine.

A sure foundation for (my) times is a wonderful promise. These
are the times that try my faith and my depth as a Christian
more than any preceding era. Yet in the midst of them, there
is a treasure to be found, and then added to my already great
store.

The fear of the Lord is the key to this treasure, Isaiah claims. I do
have a deep respect for my Lord. I admire His limitless power

110

and know that He can use it on my behalf, and does! I stand in awe of His incomparable holiness and thank Him for imputing righteousness to me as well, through His Son. I marvel at the vastness of His wisdom and trust Him to do what is right for me. I thrill to remember that He works all things together for the good of the ones who love Him. I am one of those persons. I love Him with all my heart. The promise applies to me!

I look forward to the unveiling of His plan so I can see why I was asked to walk this path of painful grief. These are heart-breaking days. These are difficult times for me. Yet there are also times when I can give testimony to His sustaining grace and power, for He generously enables me to handle one day at a time in victory.

My feet will not slip — I have *a sure foundation!*

He will be the sure foundation for your times . . . the fear of the Lord is the key to this treasure.

BE STILL, MY SOUL

"Be still, and know that I am God . . ."
PSALM 46:10A

T he challenge to *be still* appears more than once in the Bible. While it is not easily done, there is a depth of blessing and reward that ensues. The hymnwriter expressed it so beautifully:

> Be still, my soul, the Lord is on thy side;
>   Bear patiently the cross of *grief* or pain;
> Leave to thy God to order or provide;
>   In every change, He faithful will remain.
> Be still, my soul, thy best, thy heavenly Friend
>   Through thorny ways leads to a joyful end.
>
> Be still, my soul, thy God doth undertake
>   To guide the future as He has the past.
> Thy hope, thy confidence let nothing shake;
>   All now mysterious will be bright at last.
> Be still my soul, the wind and waves still know
>   His voice who ruled them while He dwelt below.

Be still, my soul, the hour is hastening on
    When we shall be forever with the Lord,
When disappointment, *grief* and fear are gone,
    Sorrow forgot, love's purest joys restored.
Be still, my soul, when change and tears are past,
    All safe and blessed we shall meet at last.

Katharina Von Schlegel

In these lyrics, grief is kept in proper perspective. I must always face my grief against the backdrop of God's love and faithfulness or it will overpower me. When it is kept in its proper place, it becomes a natural and even healthy, God-given method of dealing with my loss. My grieving period is a temporary state, painful though it is. It *cannot* destroy me — unless I permit it to!

With God's help I can face courageously the blunt realities of my great loss, confident that with God I can weather this, the blackest storm of my life. I can say to myself, *Be still, my soul, be still!* Then a new and deeper knowledge of God will sweep over me.   *

NO FANCY FOOTWORK

"We've come out of this with . . . faith intact . . . but it wasn't by any fancy footwork on our part. It was God who kept us focused on him, uncompromised."
II CORINTHIANS 1:12 THE MESSAGE

Yes, thank the Lord, I have *"come out of this with faith intact."* To deny that those days were difficult ones would be less than honest; they were among the most difficult days of my life. But to say that my faith is intact is also being honest, and it gives me a special thrill to be able to say it.

How did I do it? Well, for one thing, it was certainly not the result of any *"fancy footwork"* on my part. The credit all goes to God Who so graciously kept me focused on Himself and thus delivered me from compromising my beliefs. He strengthened my recognition of His sovereignty, even in the midst of my trial, and I am so grateful. A strong sense of God's sovereignty stabilizes us beautifully. It pleases me that He chose to give that valuable gift to me. As a result of receiving that gift of an unshakable faith in God's sovereignty, my faith is intact.

I have seen people become weary of *fancy footwork*. They have tried to maintain a close walk with God when their faith was tested, but they made that attempt in their own strength. That cannot be done successfully! They tried to step around certain questions. That is not wise. It is better to face those questions squarely.

God did not heal my honey. I asked Him to. He chose not to honor my earnest request. I face that exception to His faithfulness in fulfilling His promises head-on. I don't try to give some theological explanation. I just rest in the truth that my Sovereign Lord does all things in my best interest and in hers as well. I do not attempt to fathom the depths of His wisdom; I only bow to His sovereignty and focus on Who and What He is.

As I remind my heart of how good and how loving He is, I know with certainty that this dark valley through which we have passed together, while requiring steady plodding, needed *no fancy footwork*. The focusing of mind and heart that brought us both through in victory was a special gift from Him.   *

OUTPOURED TEARS

". . . my eyes pour out tears to God . . ."
JOB 16:20

A few minutes ago a most unexpected burst of tears
erupted unannounced. It was a special memory that
blew in like a summer tornado. Just that abruptly, the flood of
tears breached my emotional dam.

How unpredictable grief is! I was humming a happy tune a
half an hour ago. I've been doing much better lately. Then
suddenly, here grief is again with a depth and fullness that
startles and almost alarms me.

In the midst of my tears the phone rang. *Should I even
answer it? Will I be able to control my emotions if it is a person with
whom I am not willing to expose them?* — I answered. It was a
precious friend. I tried to control my tears during the
conversation, but why? What are friends for? I have even
longed for a man upon whose chest I could lay my head and
sob it all out, but there is none.

After a short loss of emotional control and gracious
acceptance of that on the part of my friend, we concluded
our conversation. I thanked the Lord for a friend who lives

so close to God that God could choose the right moment for him to phone me.

Then I asked the Lord for a verse concerning my flood of tears. I looked in Strong's Exhaustive Concordance. The third entry under "tears" caught my attention, so I looked up Job 16:20 and was thrilled with the comfort it brought my broken heart. I must also write a devotional thought on the first half of the verse. Here is the entire verse: "My intercessor is my friend as my eyes pour out tears to God." Suddenly the closeness of my dearest of all Friends became a beautiful reality and, like the disciple John, I put my head on His chest and sobbed harder than I have in a long, long time.

My Intercessor, my Friend, the Observer of my tears, I love You and I thank You that I don't have to hold anything back in Your presence. I can let my tears flow freely and fully. I am greatly comforted by Your loving concern for me.   *

MY INTERCESSOR
IS MY FRIEND!

*"My intercessor is my friend as I pour out tears to God; on behalf of a man
he pleads with God as a man pleads for his friend."*
JOB 16:20, 21

There is nothing that causes me to marvel more than the
thought of friendship with Jesus. I guess I am not the
only one who feels that way. The songwriters have expressed
their wonder repeatedly: "What a Friend we have in Jesus!"
"Friendship with Jesus, fellowship Divine; O what wonder!
How amazing! Jesus is a Friend of mine!" "I've found a
Friend, Oh, such a Friend. He loved me e'er I knew Him!"

People often remind me that they are praying for me. I
appreciate that. But the marvel of having an Intercessor Who
is my Friend Whose position is such that I feel constrained to
use capital "I", "W", "F", and "H" in this sentence when
referring to Him evokes speechless wonder from my soul.

It is wonder enough that the Lord Jesus prays for me, and
that His statement to Peter extends to me, "I have prayed for
you!" Yes, that in itself is enough to elicit awe and praise, but

to think that this Divine Intercessor is my Friend — that's almost beyond adequate commentary!

On behalf of (me) he pleads with God as a man pleads for his friend. There is a bushel of comfort to be found in those special words.

I shall do well this day in my dealing with my grief. I shall move forward in this healing process. I shall be enabled to rise up and out of my sorrow into worthwhile productiveness. I shall, by God's grace, be a blessing instead of needing to be blessed. I shall walk triumphantly through this portion of the Valley of the Shadow of Death, rejoicing in the fact that because of my Friend-Intercessor my victory is assured.

He whispers gently to my heart the same words I heard Him say to Hezekiah so long ago, *"I have seen your tears!"* I do try to hide them from others, but why try to hide them from my Friend Who sees them even when the dam holds and they do not flow from my eyes, but pour forth from my soul in a depth of inner grief? I don't have to conceal them from Him. I won't even make that futile attempt.   *

119

GOD OUR MOTHER

"As a mother comforts her child, so will I comfort you."
ISAIAH 66:13

Many years have passed since I was a little child, yet I still remember clearly what it felt like to be rocked on my mother's lap when my ear ached. I vividly recall the comfort of pressing my throbbing ear against the soothing warmth of her soft bosom while I snuggled and whimpered there.

The awfulness of my situation was ameliorated by her encircling arms. The intensity of the pain was mysteriously diminished by the rocking motion of the chair. I was right where I needed to be!

Much later in my life I find myself needing the encircling arms of my *Mother-God*. I was taught to pray, "Our Father Who art in heaven." So it is quite difficult for me to think of *God as Mother*. I can think of no other verse in the Bible where God likens Himself to a mother. This one may be unique.

The experience spoken of here is full of comfort as well as a beautiful tenderness. It is the rocking chair, earache scene.

God with infinite love and compassion offers to comfort me. No! He *promises* to!

It was Henri J.M. Nouwen who pointed out that the hands of the welcoming father in Rembrandt's *Return of the Prodigal Son* are remarkably different. The left hand is masculine and firmly presses the prodigal to the father, while the right hand is definitely feminine. It gently caresses, offering consolation and comfort. "It is a mother's hand," Nouwen insists.

In this, my moment of deep grief, I experience the tenderness of my loving God. It is the rocking chair episode repeated. I press my throbbing heart against the warmth of His comforting promises and realize afresh what a privilege it is to be a "child" of the One Who, *as a mother comforts her child," comforts me!*

As a mother comforts her child, so will I comfort you. How loving! How appealing! How gracious! How amazing! And, how very much I need that right now.

GOD MADE BOTH

"When times are good, be happy; but when times are bad, consider: God has made the one as well as the other."
ECCLESIASTES 7:14

The good times easily, gladly and joyfully elicit my praise to God. I do not thank Him for the bad times. That's an unnatural thing to do. In fact, it goes against my grain. Yet here I am reminded that *God has made the one as well as the other.*

Bad times are not enjoyable. Bitter usually has no sweetness about it. Yet things can be bittersweet. Sour is always sour — *or is it?* In a good Chinese restaurant, some of the most delectable dishes are listed on the menu as "sweet 'n sour."

Those (years) that we battled (cancer) were often characterized by bitter experiences like pain, hospitals, weakness, bone scans, blood tests, treatments, discouragement, etc. But I readily acknowledge that there was a bittersweet aspect to this period in our lives.

The sweet memories that I cherish of God-given deliverances would not be mine if we had not encountered adversities, pain and even desperately difficult times. God knew that, and in His loving wisdom He permitted our bad times. I can somewhat readily acknowledge that God *permitted* the difficulty, but this verse goes beyond that. It reminds me that He *made* the bad times. That's hard for me to swallow.

I notice, though, that while I am told to be happy when times are good, I am not asked to be happy when times are bad. I am only asked to *consider that* <u>*God has made the one as well as the other*</u>.

I must ask myself the question that Job asked, "Shall I accept good from God, and not trouble?" (Job 2:10) No, by His grace, I will accept both. On either kind of day, I will say, "This is the day the Lord has made; I will rejoice and be glad in it" (Ps. 118:24).

When times are good, be happy; but when times are bad, consider: <u>*God made the one as well as the other*</u>.

FALLING APART?

"Even though on the outside it often looks like things are falling apart on us, on the inside, where God is making new life, not a day goes by without his unfolding grace."
II CORINTHIANS 4:16   THE MESSAGE

How easy it is to feel as if everything has *fallen apart* on me! My plans have been thwarted. My dreams have been shattered. My world has disintegrated. These are statements based upon some undeniable facts, but they are not the ones I should dwell on. There is another side to this coin of truth. In this instance it is the *in*-side!

God is doing a work of grace *on the inside* at the same time that things have *fallen apart* on the outside. I will never forget that. My perspective can so easily become distorted if I look at my circumstances instead of looking at my Lord.

Nothing has steadied me more during this dark and sometimes even frightening walk through the Valley of the Shadow of Death than my strong belief in the sovereignty of God. I know this with a profound certainty: my Heavenly Father does all things well.

So, I find great comfort in a statement like this one that Paul makes. Deep in my heart I do know that *on the inside* God is building up, even while *on the outside* things have crumbled. I am profoundly aware that *"not a day goes by without His unfolding grace."*

My task during these difficult months is to cultivate a strong ability to hear, so that God's "gentle whisper" can get through to me. Then I can be cheered, encouraged and built up, in spite of the external tearing down.

God's purposes have not been temporarily stalled — not for a single day! No! *"Not a day goes by without His unfolding grace."*

Such a confidence keeps my little boat on a steady, preordained course throughout this awful storm. There is no danger of capsizing, or of being swamped by the waves of grief that dash over my prow so mercilessly and relentlessly. While my grief cannot be denied, neither can it do me in — not if I keep these truths in focus.   *

HIS DEEP LOVE

". . . because of his deep love and concern for you, you should practice
tenderhearted mercy and kindness to others."
COLOSSIANS 3:12B THE LIVING BIBLE

N obody ever loved me more deeply and dearly than my
sweetheart! I don't think I took that for granted,
either. I reciprocated with a consistency of love that I
remember joyously now.

I sorely miss having someone to love so deeply, and to
love me deeply in return. God made me to love and be loved.
I know there are lots of people who love me. Some love me
dearly. But it is not the same — it cannot be.

So, do I sit and brood over a loss that cannot in this life be
regained? No! I do something about it. What? The
instructions are clear: I am to *practice tenderhearted mercy and
kindness to others.* That part of me that lavished tenderhearted
kindness on others, and especially on my sweetheart, is not to
be allowed to atrophy.

Last night I telephoned the home of friends who are
facing surgery. Our bond of friendship and love was
strengthened; I sensed it. Leon thanked me warmly more

than once for phoning. And why should I not call? They called me so faithfully 'to see me through my grief-walk. I deeply appreciate their friendship. Friendship is a two-way street; I must lovingly do my part. I must show to them the same kind of love they have shown me.

I think this passage actually goes beyond that. It speaks of an initiating love and tenderness toward people who have not shown it to me. Yesterday I met a man at the gas station who has brought a lot of pain and heartache to my life. In love I reached out to him, and the response was very positive! There is something very potent in tenderhearted mercy and kindness.

No love expressed has ever duplicated the profound love and concern my Savior has shown to me. Not even the love of my honey to me, nor mine for her. *"The love of God is greater far than tongue or pen can ever tell."*   *

MY FRAGRANCE

"While the king was at his table, my perfume spread its fragrance . . .
awake north wind, and come, south wind! Blow on my garden, that
its fragrance may spread abroad."
SONG OF SOLOMON 1:12, 4:16

My *perfume* and *my fragrance* are both spoken of here. It is
easy to forget that there is a fragrance that exudes
from my life when it is totally committed to Christ. I have
enjoyed that sweet fragrance emanating from others, but
quite appropriately have not recognized it in myself.

The first of these two verses indicates that fellowship
releases *fragrance*, for it is while the King sits at the table with
me that *my fragrance* spreads. The second one implies that both
trouble and triumph release *fragrance*, for it is the *north wind and
the south wind* that spread it abroad.

The *south winds* have always been most welcome, but these
north winds I find difficult to take. I have never been able to
pray the prayer, *"Awake, north wind, and come, south wind! Blow
on my garden."* But I do not have to pray that prayer to
experience the dual winds of adversity and prosperity — they
come uninvited.

The winds that are blowing on my garden right now are from the north. Shall I lament them? Or shall I invite them to cause the fragrance of my garden to be spread abroad?

Some fragrances are released by warm winds that cause the blossoms to open and the fragrance to emanate. Some fragrances are released when the harsh, cold winds bruise and crush, and in the process the fragrance is released. The mint that grows by the side of my house is extra fragrant when I take a leaf between thumb and forefinger and crush it, or at least bruise it. As the north winds bruise and attempt to crush me, may it please God to let a fragrance be released from within me.

"Awake, north wind, and come, south wind! Blow on my garden that its fragrance may spread abroad."

HOLIDAY COURAGE

"David found courage in the LORD his God."
I SAMUEL 30:6B

S ometimes I feel I need a great deal of courage to face the future alone. We faced everything together and it halved our burdens and doubled our joys. Those wonderful days are history now and I must find new sources of courage and consultation.

When David was facing a situation where he felt very much alone, we are told that he *found courage in the Lord, his God.* I like that. I can do it too!

I need courage to go face a couples' world. I don't really like waiting at a banquet to see if there's a table with a single place remaining, so I won't take the space of two. I notice that most tables are deliberately arranged to accommodate multiples of two. As uncomfortable as this is, I still refuse to withdraw and not venture out into a couple's world I will take courage in the Lord my God and go where I am not fully comfortable.

I don't like facing holidays. They used to be such happy times together. Thanksgiving, Christmas, Valentine's Day,

Mother's Day, birthdays, and our anniversary — all are days I dread now. Yet, the Lord can give a special grace for those days.

"David found courage in the Lord his God." I am inspired by that. He is a role model for me, and I intend to follow his example. Even holidays with their ability to compound grief are no match for God's gracious outpourings of love. My predicament is nowhere near as difficult as David's was. In the midst of his horrible situation he *found courage in the Lord, his God.*

Surely for my less traumatic and dramatic circumstances of life I can do the same. We are assured that the supply of grace for our need flows from "His riches in glory by Christ Jesus." He is always ready to give a bountiful supply of grace, even for holidays. On the basis of such a positive and firm knowledge of my loving God, I plan to take courage in Him whenever I am faced with anything where aloneness makes me uncomfortable and in need of a boost to my morale.   *

THE REFINER'S FIRE

". . . he knows the way that I take; when he has tested me, I will
come forth as gold."
JOB 23:10

The *way that I take* is not a pleasant trail. No one even
tries to convince me that it is, thankfully. People
sometimes say bizarre things in their attempts to be kind and
helpful, but they don't try to convince me that this path is
without thornbushes. Some can only imagine what it is like
until they also hike these trails, and unfortunately, they will!

There is a lot of comfort, however, in knowing that this
path is known to Jesus. He knows it well — intimately, in
fact. He has walked it ever so many times before. No true
Christian has ever walked it alone. His promise is, "I am with
you always," and that promise He has faithfully kept with
every Christian who has been called upon to traverse this
painful trail.

I need to develop more God-consciousness. "He walks
with me and He talks with me, and He tells me I am His own
. . ." Those are familiar and beautiful words, but now I must
translate them into my present circumstances so that I will

not feel so all alone at times. When I am lonely it is because I have temporarily lost my God-consciousness.

The Comforter is also <u>the Refiner</u>. That is not a difficult concept. When my children were small I was both the disciplining dad and the fond father at the same time. My Heavenly Father, Who knows the way that I am taking, and is walking with me through it, is working faithfully to refine my gold. He is making my life into something precious and eternally valuable, something fit for a King, something pure as <u>the refining fire</u> does its work and the dross is consumed.

How sad if I walk this trail of tears and do not come out of it a better person! I need a deep inner confidence concerning the dual facts that I shall come out of this and that I shall be as refined gold. It is not a matter of "if" but "when" ("... *when He has tested me* ..."). I feel certain that the *when* of it varies from individual to individual. I only care that when I do come out of this trial I am, at last, as refined gold and very valuable to Him.

BATTERED BUT NOT
DEMORALIZED

*"We've been surrounded and battered by troubles, but we're not
demoralized; . . . we've been thrown down, but we
haven't broken."*
II CORINTHIANS 4:8 THE MESSAGE

That describes me perfectly! My troubles have indeed
both surrounded and *battered* me. Sometimes my spirit
feels so bruised. *But* I am *not demoralized*. I can still sense that
His perfect plan for my life, though beyond my capacity to
comprehend it, or even to welcome it, is good. Somehow it is
good.

I also feel as if I have been *thrown down*, but I know that I
have not broken. He has to reach down and pick me up, but
He does not have to pick up the pieces! I am surviving this
pain — with God's help I am. I am continuing to want to
live, though there is so much less to live for now that my
sweetheart has been taken out of my life for awhile.

The temporary nature of the separation is comforting. The
truth of the matter is that it may be a very short separation,
for the return of the Savior seems very near. So many things

point to the imminent reappearing of the Lord Jesus. When I ponder that, my heart cries out, *"Even so, come quickly, Lord Jesus!"* Yes, I want to live, but I would far rather live there than here. I welcome the return of the Savior. I do not wish my present life away, for just as my honey accomplished God's full plan for *her* life, so I want Him to do with my life.

So, while I serve, and work, and wait I must rejoice in the fact that while I have been *battered* by what was happening, I have *not* been *demoralized*; and while I am *thrown down*, I am *not broken*. I am still useful to my Lord, and I will with holy determination serve Him well in any way that I can. I do not deny my bruised condition. I only rejoice over the way He is bringing me through the darkest valley of my life and will most certainly continue to do that. One day my bruises will begin to fade away. Some day there will remain no visible reminders of the *battering* I have endured. Deep within my spirit, I *know* that!

JESUS IS PAINTING A PICTURE

"We are transformed in ever increasing splendour into his own image, and this is the work of the Lord . . ."
II CORINTHIANS 3:18 PHILLIPS MODERN ENGLISH

Heather, a sweet little three and one-half year old, looked up into her mother's face and said so seriously, "Jesus is painting a picture of me, and He isn't finished yet." I cried when I first read that.

I remember so well the evening when Jesus finished painting my sweetheart's portrait and she was given permission to step down from the pose she had struck. Perhaps I should say "up" for at that precious moment she stepped *up* into His glorious Presence.

Upon hearing the sweet statement Heather made, I realized immediately that His portrait of me is not completed as yet. I go on with life, and He is watching constantly, while with sure strokes He paints my picture. I am a painter, too. I know how the artist's eyes glance back and forth continually from the subject to the canvas.

Lord Jesus, I want to handle my grief and live my life in such a manner that what You paint is a thing of beauty, of strength, of character. " . . . we know that suffering produces perseverance; perseverance, character; and character, hope. And hope does not disappoint us . . . " (Romans 5:3b-5a).

Help me day by day to draw upon Your strength, to look into Your face and to feed upon Your manna so that I am continually being changed into Your likeness. I want my portrait to bear a strong "family resemblance." I want everyone to know that I am a joint-heir with You. I want them to know that You and I have the same Father. I want them to see that Father in me, just as they see Him when they see You!

To Phillip You said, "Anyone who has seen me has seen the Father" (John 14:9). My lofty goal, Lord Jesus, is to be able to say that too. That does not seem to me to be sacrilegious. I feel it is exactly what You are wanting of me, and for me. By the way, it is an oil painting, Lord Jesus, isn't it? (So You can easily scrape away the old image and repaint as I become more and more like You.)

I HAVE PLANS FOR YOU

"I know the plans I have for you . . . plans to prosper you and not to harm
you, plans to give you a hope and a future."
JEREMIAH 29:11

T hank You, Lord, for these reassuring words.
Sometimes it is difficult to think of the future, let alone
to deliberately face it. We walked together. We completed
each other. We served You together. Now half of me is gone.
I do not feel whole any more. When I try to make plans, I
find little heart for the exercise — little confidence in my
decisions. That will change. I know that. But for the present I
really needed to hear these promises, reassuring me that *You*
have a set of plans that are positive and profitable and full of
hope. I like that!

You have always had a perfect plan for my life. I was
willing to accept that fact, but not really willing to accept the
part that included amputation. That has been the most
painful thing for me. It has been a cup with a strong, bitter,
and very distasteful flavor. I cannot deny that. You drank a
bitter cup for me! You were a Man of Sorrows and
acquainted with grief so early in life. My dark valley was

delayed. There is great comfort in realizing that You, Who Yourself staggered through this painful valley, traversing it in triumph, have designed a future for me full of hope.

Help me to rest in the truth that You know the future You have designed for me, and that is enough. I do not have to know it too. All I have to know is that You are loving and good and gentle and caring. I am also comforted by knowing that You are all-powerful and can bring to pass everything You have planned. I can even get excited when I stop to think of what those plans might include! You have given me more than a hint when You use such words as *prosper* and *hope*. I have been very satisfied with the wonderful extras You planned in my past, so why should I expect any less in the future? I await with expectant heart the unfolding of Your beautiful plan. I can trust the blueprint You have drafted for me.   *

I HAVE SEEN YOUR TEARS

"I have heard your prayer and seen your tears."
II KINGS 20:5

These words bring special comfort to me, dear Lord. My tears are close to the surface today for no apparent reason, other than the depth of my grief.

Today is not an anniversary. Nothing that I am aware of has happened to trigger these tears. Grief doesn't seem to need a reason other than the loss which is undeniably there. Grief walks into my day unannounced, uninvited, unwelcome, and sometimes at moments when I least expect it.

The longer I walk through this desolate, dark valley, the more alone with God I feel. Loved ones and friends are not as willing to speak of my honey as they were in the days immediately following her home-going. That reminds me of a song that I have loved for many years. The thoughts expressed in it I must now put into practice:

Alone with God, blest the hours I spend,
In divinest fellowship

With my Lord and Friend!
Heaven seems to open wide
    At His blessed side, and my soul is satisfied,
    When I'm alone with God.

Unknown

It is not necessarily burdensome that I walk more and more alone, as long as it is *alone with God*. I am never really alone — *never*! "No, never alone. No, never alone. He promised never to leave me, never to leave me alone," (Ludie D. Pickett) another gospel song insists.

Even when I feel like I am all alone, <u>He sees my tears</u> and He hears any prayer I lift to Him. So I must learn on days like this to "tell it to Jesus." (I am recalling so many appropriate gospel songs today!) "Are you weary? Are you heavy hearted? Tell it to Jesus. *Tell it to Jesus.* You've no other, such a friend or brother. Tell it to Jesus alone." (Edmund S. Lorenz)

That's good advice. On this emotionally unstable day, when waves of loneliness are sweeping over me, I'll just *tell it to Jesus*, and I'll hear His tender response: "*I have heard your prayer and seen your tears.*" Then I will no longer feel all alone with my grief; instead Divine comfort will flood my soul, bringing with it songs, like these I have quoted. *

RULING PEACE

"Let the peace of Christ rule in your hearts."
COLOSSIANS 3:15

The thought of having peace reign instead of grief or fear or circumstances is a very pleasant prospect. *The peace of Christ* is a priceless commodity and quite supernatural.

Jesus referred to it and bequeathed it to me under the most difficult circumstances, when He said, "Peace I leave with you; my peace I give you" (John 14:27a). Those words were spoken in the shadow of the cross. With the worst experiences of His life only hours away, He spoke of a peace that passes understanding. And, He was not just talking about it — He was passing it on to me!

This peace is able to keep both my heart and my mind in amazing, unnatural tranquility in the midst of threatening circumstances. It is the same peace that enabled Paul and Silas to sing at midnight with their hands and feet in the stocks, inside a prison. Circumstances, no matter how bleak, cannot squelch the song of the victorious soul.

There's a peace in my heart
That the world never gave,
A peace *it cannot take away!*

Though the trials of life
May surround like a cloud,
I've a peace that has come there *to stay!*

All the world seemed to sing
Of a Savior and King,
When peace sweetly came to my heart.

Troubles all fled away,
And my night turned to day.
Blessed Jesus, how glorious Thou art!

Mrs. Will L. Murphy

Yes, He is constantly abiding with me, and there is indeed an element of rapture Divine in that. His "oh, so kind" whisper of the words "I will never leave Thee" ministers a deep and abiding peace that is alien to this world. I must be careful to *let the peace of Christ rule in my heart.* *

ONE DAY AT A TIME

"God will take care of your tomorrow . . . Live <u>one day at a time</u>."
MATTHEW 6:34 THE LIVING BIBLE

The expression *Live <u>one day at a time</u>* has become so common that I forget it is not just a trite twenty-first century piece of advice. God spoke those words through Matthew centuries ago.

I have been living *<u>one day at a time</u>* and finding grace for each new day. God's own provision of "hidden manna" has been all I have needed to sustain me, even on the darkest days. Well-known promises have become foundational truths that let me stand tall and strong even on difficult days. "As your days, so shall your strength be" has been newly proven every twenty-four hours!

<u>One day at a time</u>. That's how I'm handling it, but when I apply the *<u>one day at a time</u>* principle to my living, I must not forget the other half of the verse: *God will take care of your tomorrow.*

All my tomorrows are in His hand. He knows right now what each will be like and exactly what I will need. All my todays are in His hand, too! It seems as if the days are flying past. Time is a strange thing — sometimes it flies and sometimes it drags, in spite of a scientific constancy that is precise. My times are in His hands. My todays, my tomorrows; that is my comfort.

So I live _one_ _day_ _at_ _a_ _time_ committing my tomorrows to my compassionate, loving Heavenly Father, remembering that He will take care of all of my times as I simply commit them to Him — even my every moment!

Moment by moment I'm kept in His love;
   Moment by moment I've life from above;
Looking to Jesus till glory doth shine;
   Moment by moment, O Lord, I am Thine.

D. W. Whittle

I will remember with joy that God will take care of (my) tomorrow, and I'll just live _one day at a time_.

THE VALLEY OF BERACAH

". . . they assembled . . . in the Valley of Beracah . . . there they blessed the
LORD; therefore the name of the place was called the Valley of
Beracah . . ."
II CHRONICLES 20:26

Beracah! That name means, "Blessing"! If I think of
valleys as representing my difficult times in life, and
mountaintops representing my thrilling answers to prayer and
other wonderful experiences, then this "valley" has a most
inappropriate name.

The Valley of the Shadow of Death has always seemed
dark and foreboding, *and it is*. In many ways it is worse than I
had ever imagined. But there is another truth that, when
superimposed over that one, works wonders! It is the truth
that even the darkest of valleys can be transformed by the
power of the living God into a place of praise and blessing.
That takes a miracle of His doing, certainly, but He is a God
of miracles! And He is the Lord of every valley. Fenelon,
commenting on the passage that tells of an incredible victory
God gave the Israelites over the Syrians notes that the big
mistake those Syrians made was in assuming that God was

146

only the God of the hills, and not the God of the valleys as well (see I Kings 20:23). He insists, "We make that same mistake." *He is right!*

In my bright times, when "everything's goin' my way," it is easy for me to praise the Lord. In my dark hours I don't really feel like praising, even though friends may glibly say, "Praise the Lord anyhow!" I think, "*You haven't been here. You don't know what it's like.*" But in this passage I am made to realize that God has the power to change the name of *any* valley to <u>*The Valley of Beracah*</u>. When He did it in this instance, it had been perhaps the darkest valley Judah and their king, Jehoshaphat, had ever encountered. A "great multitude" had come against them and they were terribly afraid. But God worked for them, slaying their enemy. They did nothing but sing and praise the beauty of holiness and *God fought the battle for them.* Judah didn't have to lift a finger!

I need to have God fight this battle for me. I know that He can win it resoundingly — not just barely!

O Lord, please help me to be able to rename the Valley of the Shadow of Death <u>*the Valley of Beracah*</u>. You can do that for me. I know You can!

No Sitting on My Hands!

". . . get out there and walk — better yet, run! — on the road God called you to travel. I don't want any of you sitting around on your hands. I don't want anyone strolling off, down some path that goes nowhere . . . do this with humility and discipline — not in fits and starts, but steadily, pouring yourselves out for each other in acts of love . . ."
EPHESIANS 4:1-3 THE MESSAGE

Though I do not really feel like "running" yet, I *can* walk. And I will! I will walk the walk of faith. This is the road *God called me to travel.* I would never have chosen it for myself. This road is far too painful for me to make a deliberate choice to travel on it. God in His wisdom has chosen it for me. I must not only accept it, but I must also learn to walk on it well, and even to begin running eventually.

I must never lose sight of purposeful living. Grief has its own dangers. I can become so self-centered and self-concerned that I cease to be useful to God and end up *sitting on my hands.* I don't want that to happen.

I like the idea of *pouring out myself for others in acts of love.* Despite the fact that I am alone now, I can still do that. We did it together for all those years, the two of us. But that's not altogether true! The truth is that we did it together, the three of us! Now I can still do it "together" with just the two of us. He never really asks me to do anything alone. He said, "Lo, I am with you always." No, I haven't been *sitting on my hands*; I have been active for Him. I realize that there is healing value in worthwhile activity, especially selfless activity.

I am well aware that there are *paths that go nowhere*. I don't ever want to be doing my walking on one of those! By God's grace and with His help, I will make the years that remain to me, and even the tears that remain to me, to be useful and for His glory. I will endeavor to make each day count. I will do my part in the way of "physical therapy" following this amputation, but I will put my trust in Him for the healing. *I will not sit on my hands*. I will *walk*, and then I will *run* on this road.   *

FATHER, I WANT . . .

". . . Father, I want those you have given me to be with me where I am, and to see my glory . . . "
JOHN 17:24

My poor grieving heart wants my sweetheart to be with me where I am, but there I must stop the sentence. The statement the Lord Jesus made is very different. He wanted it for my honey's sake; I want it for my own lonely sake.

Oh, I would never want my sweetheart back to a life of suffering. My love for her is deeper than that. But I cannot help wishing that we could still be together. I am well aware that the separation is temporary. The day will come when the prayer of the Lord Jesus will be fulfilled for me, too, even as it has already been for her.

Somehow, hearing afresh the earnest prayer of my dear Savior regarding His desires to have us be with Him helps me to accept the early departure of my honey. It cannot totally remove my pain, but it can help me put in perspective what has happened.

Lord Jesus, one of the ways that I can lighten my grief is by reminding my heart of precious truths like this. I respect the longings of Your great heart of love and I am willing for You to shower upon my sweetheart the revelation of Your glory. I remember her soft weeping as she described that beautiful vision You gave to her one night when she was so ill. My sweetheart was not one to have visions. I don't think she ever had another, before nor since, but the description of the glories of the entryway to Heaven were so precious and indescribably beautiful that I would be selfish to deny her that dream becoming a reality. I wept with her as she recounted it in detail, struggling to find vocabulary that would even come near to describing adequately the magnificent walk down those glorious corridors' that You prematurely permitted her. It was a foretaste for her of the glory You so deeply wanted to have Your followers enjoy.

I get the distinct impression that You can hardly wait for us to come to You. I understand now that the death of Your saints is precious in Your sight! (Psalm 116:15, KJV).

SOMETIME WE'LL
UNDERSTAND

"We'll see it all then, see it all as clearly as God sees us . . ."
DEUTERONOMY 23:7A

S ometimes I feel there is no one to whom I can talk who
would understand some of the questions that persist in
my mind. There are things I just do not understand. Oh, it is
not that my faith is shaken or that I am struggling to maintain
a spiritual stance. It is rather that some of the beautiful clichés
people use just do not affect me the way they expect them to.
I play along with their game, but I do not respond well to
thoughts like "It's so marvelous for her," or "Just think of
what she is enjoying over there!" I don't really know what she
is experiencing over there, and when I try to imagine I often
stop trying. I cannot explain my feelings to others. I keep
thinking, "They cannot understand. How can they? I cannot
understand myself."

There is some comfort for me in a hymn I have known for
many years, but never really comprehended before:

Not now, but in the coming years,
　　It may be in the better land,
I'll read the meaning of my tears,
　　And there, _sometime, I'll understand._

I'll catch the broken thread again,
　　And finish what I here began;
Heaven will the mysteries explain,
　　And then, ah then, I'll understand.

I'll know why clouds instead of sun
　　Were over many a cherished plan
Why song has ceased when scarce begun;
　　'Tis there, _sometime, I'll understand._

I'll trust in God through all my days;
　　I will not fear, He holds my hand!
Though dark my way, I'll sing and praise,
　　"Sometime, _sometime I'll understand._"
　　　　(personalization mine)

Maxwell N. Cornelius

For me, that's the best way to handle the things I do not understand. I must commit them to the Lord and remind my heart that,

I'll see it all then, see it all as clearly as God sees me.

ABSOLUTE SOVEREIGNTY

"Exactly as I say it, I have it happen. Just as I plan, I do it."
ISAIAH 46:11B

There is no equivocating here. God is saying that everything happens in conjunction with His sovereignty — His *absolute sovereignty*. There is great comfort in that thought for me.

I shall live until what God has planned for me to do is completed. And even when I reach that point of departure, it will be exciting! That's when I will begin the next incomparably glorious phase of my eternal existence. So, the clever statement I have heard repeated so often, "A Christian is immortal until his life's work is done," is only a half-truth. True Christians are, in one sense, immortal eternally, for they shall never die other than the shadow-death that is a part of this temporary, fleeting life.

That death (of the body) pales in significance when we recognize its limitations. It can touch *only* the body! God is in complete control of both body and soul. He is also in control of this day. He will be in control not only of tomorrow, but also of *all* my tomorrows. I have not a thing to fear. In God's sovereignty, He decided that my honey would precede me into the next absolutely perfect phase of eternal life in Christ. I can only try to imagine what that is like for her.

The fact of the matter is that, the way time is flying, soon we will both be enjoying a freedom we never knew here. I fully expect to share it with her in every aspect. We have loved to travel here, and I think we shall enjoy it even more there. There will be no congested Miami airport to frustrate and even frighten us. There will be no long layovers, waiting for the next plane. There will be no language barriers. There will be no weariness, or weakness, or jet lag. There will be no thieves to be wary of, and no rough roads to distress.

Yes, there is a great day coming! I don't have to speculate as to when or how, for God has said this: *Exactly as I say it, I have it happen. Just as I plan, I do it.* I rest in that, content to trust in His *absolute sovereignty*.

THE MAIN THING

*"When the time comes, we'll be plenty ready to exchange exile for
homecoming. But neither exile nor homecoming is the main thing.
Cheerfully pleasing God is the main thing, and that's what we aim to do,
regardless of our conditions."*
II CORINTHIANS 5:8, 9 THE MESSAGE

It is difficult to keep a proper perspective while I am
grieving. I have work to do for the Lord and I want to do
it well. I don't want to be so immersed in my grief that I fail
to accomplish His plan for me. I remain here on earth
because my own work is not yet complete. I don't want to fall
into the error of getting things so out of focus that I am not
usable.

I recall a dear "saint" who came to our Fairhaven Retreat
Center for recuperation when she was exhausted. I enjoyed
counseling her. She had so much spiritual wisdom.
Sometimes I felt like I was the counselee! One day she said,
"*The main thing* is to keep *the main thing the main thing*!" I had
never heard that before, and it impressed me. Looking at my
busy life, I realized quickly that I often put trivial tasks ahead

of the main ones. I needed to learn to do the important first, the trivial later.

Paul says that cheerfully pleasing God is _the main thing_. I really do want to please Him — even while I am grieving.

I know He does not deny me my tears, nor expect me to act super-spiritual, as if nothing has happened. I also know that He wants me to be sensitive to His new assignments for me. I have work to do for Him. I trust He was pleased with how long I took searching for the right card for Donna Leitzke. Steve was suddenly taken from her. That means she will have to rear their five children alone! I searched and searched until I found one that was just right. I remember clearly the text, "There are no appropriate words for a time like this; I only hope it helps to know I care." I would have bought a dozen for future use if there had been duplicates, but there weren't any.

Whether it is choosing a card, or serving at church, or sending a copy of this book to someone who is grieving, I want to please Him cheerfully, keeping _the main thing — the main thing._   *

NEW LIFE BURGEONS

"The old life is gone; a new life burgeons!"
II CORINTHIANS 5:17

How appropriate these words are, even out of their beautiful context! I have to face the fact that my old life is gone. That's forever settled now. Nothing will bring it back. What a significant milestone when I can begin to perceive that a new life is burgeoning!

Today I bought hanging baskets of flowers at Walmart's. They had been $5 each and were reduced to $1 each! I bought twelve of them to adorn the open archways of the large, new gazebo I had erected on the Fairhaven campus as a memorial to my sweetheart. Tonight I cut the tall spindly stalks back. Down at the bottom of each cluster of straggly begonia there is *new life burgeoning*. That beautiful new growth was hardly even visible until I cut away all those skinny, tall stalks. I am so very pleased with the finished product. I put Miracle Gro plant food on them. I will give them the TLC they need, and in two or three weeks they will be very attractive. And I will enjoy them all the more because they were 80% off the original price!

It is time for me to cut away some of the old growth that keeps _new life_ from _burgeoning_ in me. As much as possible I must begin to keep my grief under control, rather than letting it control me. When I became so worn-out during the long caregiving period and I would hear myself saying, "I'm not going to make it!" I would say to myself (right out loud), "Change that tape!" Now, when I begin to mentally review those difficult days, it is time to say again, "Change that tape!"

There certainly are cheerier tapes I can play. I can recall with joy (instead of with tears) the happy times we had together. I can remember the many years we did share instead of lamenting that we are not sharing this one. I can cut away the spindly overgrowth, and discover that underneath it all there really is _new life burgeoning_! I can feed it, encourage it and give it the TLC it needs to become a thing of beauty again. I can — and I will!   *

DAILY BURDEN BEARER

"Praise be to the Lord, to God our Savior, who <u>daily bears</u>
<u>our burdens</u>."
PSALM 68:19

What a deep comfort it is to realize that *every* day —
each new day — the Lord lovingly <u>bears my burdens</u>. I
think of Him as the Great Burden Bearer, but perhaps I have
not thought about the fact that He so faithfully continues that
ministry to my heart — day after day after burden-filled day.

I cared for my sweetheart's needs daily, and counted it a
great privilege and joy to be able to serve her. I know she
would have done the same for me. I never thought of that
loving care as a burden, but rather as a privilege and an
opportunity to fulfill promises I had made to her nearly forty
years earlier at a sacred altar.

His care for me is a fulfillment of promises He made to
me a long time ago, too. "I will never leave you nor forsake
you," He promised when I became His adopted child. "I have
loved you with an everlasting love" is His reassurance to my
heart. I can only marvel that He should love me so, for I do

160

not see in myself anything that is worthy of such a depth of loving.

When I was a child, a song that was frequently sung in our church expressed the question that welled up in my young heart as I meditated upon the great love of the Lord Jesus for me,

> *Why* should He love me so?
>> Why should He love *me* so?
>>> Why should my Savior to Calvary go?
>>> Why should He love me so?
>
> Robert Harkness

It was more than a song to me — it was an honest question that I asked in worshipful amazement. I don't know why, but I do know that He loves me dearly and deeply. Out of that great depth of love, He *daily bears my burdens*, just as He promised.

The spontaneous response that flows from my appreciative heart is, *Praise be to the Lord, to God my Savior, Who daily bears my burdens.*

ALL GAIN? – NO LOSS?

"You let the distress bring you to God, not drive you from him. The result was all gain, no loss."
II CORINTHIANS 7:9 THE MESSAGE

There are events in life which clearly move us in one direction or another. I find this introduction to deep grief difficult to categorize. I honestly do not feel it has *driven me from Him*, but I cannot with certainty say that it has moved me closer to Him.

However, as I try to analyze my condition, I realize that God has spoken to me more frequently, and to my surprise has spoken through me more powerfully. I can recall even saying to myself, "Whatever it is, I don't want to lose it!" So I guess the distress has moved me toward God, without my having some big perception of it.

I know my heart in this. I sincerely want to be better and not bitter. I want to be closer, not colder. My Heavenly Father knows that.

Perhaps the lack of perception of moving closer is in some way related to the numbness of all other feelings. That appears to be an integral part of the grief package. Grief looms so large that it inundates the emotional landscape and makes it difficult to enjoy anything at first. I remember how obviously true that was right after my honey's death. I totally lost the pleasure capacity. Even food had no enjoyable taste for the first two weeks! Thankfully that capacity has returned completely.

Is it possible that even the ability to enjoy and appreciate God was numbed for a time, and though in some ways I was moving closer to Him, I was not even aware of it? I want to feel His Presence very close to me. He has promised that as I draw near to Him, He will in turn draw near to me.

Please, Lord, enlarge my capacity for feeling. From a child I have followed the "better not bitter" approach to the heartaches of life. I certainly don't want to change now. I want to perceive the *gain* of it all. Right now it is easier to see the *loss* big and clear and to be somewhat numb when it comes to experiencing Your Presence.   *

A TIME TO MOURN

*"There is a time for everything, and a season for every activity under heaven
. . . a time to mourn . . ."*
ECCLESIASTES 3:1, 4

Grieving *takes* time! I am so thankful God says what He does in this passage. He gives me written permission to mourn.

But how much time does grieving take? Who can tell? The books I have read sometimes speak with too much authority about what I can expect, yet they all acknowledge that no two people grieve alike!

I have friends who are healing much more quickly than I am. Are they more spiritual? Are they right and am I wrong, or am I right and they are wrong? No! There is no wrong or right about it; there is just difference. I go with the flow of my own grief and neither judge nor envy. I just know that my troubled heart does not seem to do much responding as yet to the things that should enable me to get past my pain. This is *my time to mourn*.

My sweetheart is not just a memory. I loved her with all my heart. At the very same time I loved the Lord Jesus with all my heart. That tells me that the day could come when He would bring to me yet another to love with all my heart, but that cannot be forced. It must come in His time. Yes, in His time. For now she is " . . . my sweetheart, my only sweetheart. She made me happy when skies were gray." But my earnest prayers, "Please, don't take my sweetheart away" did not avail, and she is gone for awhile.

I'll grieve as long as I must, and nobody can tell me when enough is enough — nobody but God, that is. *There is . . . a time to mourn,* and for my grieving heart that is still the present.

God will help me as I walk through this unavoidable section of the Valley of the Shadow of Death. I can no longer hold my honey's hand, but I can recognize the strong hand of the Savior as He slips it into mine, dispelling much of the gloom in this dark passageway.   *

A WATER PILLOW!

". . . every night my pillow is wet with tears."
PSALM 6:6 THE LIVING BIBLE

The longer I grieve, the more private my tears become. No one knows how frequently I cry. I am almost afraid to be open about it, especially with people who have not lost someone this dear to them. They might think it is high time I showed some healing, especially if I am the strong, spiritual person they had thought me to be!

A friend of mine wrote, "I am not the Bill Johnson you thought you knew!" He is condemning himself for being unable to pull himself together the way he thinks he should. Oh yes, he is the Bill I knew! He is as human as I am, and when he writes, "I am devastated!" he has no idea that he is bringing comfort to me. I am devastated, too. It reassures me when I realize that there are other dedicated Christians who feel the same devastation that I do.

David talked about his pillow being wet with tears nightly. It's normal! I haven't even looked up the setting of this Psalm to find out what he was crying about. It is enough to read of his nightly weeping. That's partly why I like him so much —

166

he was as human as I am; and though he was the great King of Israel, he was willing to reveal that humanity. David transparently verbalized what I feel.

No, I don't cry nightly, but there are nights when I do cry — hard! I try to remember at those times the picturesque words of Augustine, written in the fifth century, "The tears … streamed down and I let them flow as freely as they would, making of them *a pillow for my heart*. On them it rested."

Now, that's real victory, when I can make of my tears *a pillow for my heart* to rest upon! Some people really *love* a water bed. They rave about the extra comfort it provides for their back. So, couldn't *a water pillow* provide extraordinary comfort for my heart?! I will not lament my lamentation. By God's grace I will learn to let my tears do something more than to wet my pillow. In place of a watered pillow, I shall have *a water pillow*. There my heart shall rest.

YOU WILL COMFORT ME

"Though you have made me see troubles, many and bitter, you will restore my life again . . . You will . . . comfort me once again."
PSALM 71:20, 21

There is an upbeat, strong note of assurance in these words that I love! It grows out of a knowledge of the nature of the Almighty. He is loving and gracious and caring.

He wept at the grave of Lazarus. He consistently had compassion on those who were suffering. He worked relentlessly to alleviate the heartaches of the people when He walked this earth in human form in the Person of the Lord Jesus.

He will work to assuage my grief — *He surely will!* He *has*, in fact. I am doing better than I was earlier in this process. I am slowly healing and coming through it. The day will come when my tears will be rare instead of so common. That will not mean I have forgotten my sweetheart. No, it will mean that I have adjusted to her being there waiting for me, and I here waiting to join her. It will mean that the wound caused by our separation has healed and I have gone on with life,

168

seeking to please both Him and her by the way I accept my lot and continue to make the most of my life.

Yes, the troubles were *many* and they were very *bitter* — I cannot deny that. The cup from which I drank was the most bitter one of my entire life. But I shall not dwell upon those bitter dregs. By the grace of God I shall look forward instead of backward. As I do that, *God will comfort me* as He promised.

God of all comfort, I have every confidence that the weeping which has endured through this long night of my grief will dissipate, and joy shall come in the morning (Psalm 30:5). There are already joyous moments. I can laugh sometimes. I can see the humor in things. I can enjoy the springtime and smell the flowers. There will come a new springtime in my soul as this winter fades away, and as You fulfill Your promise of comforting me again. I know that. And because I know it with such deep assurance, my spirit is filled with a most welcome hope.   *

GOD'S FOOTPRINTS

". . . though <u>Your footprints were not seen</u>, You led Your people . . . "
PSALM 77:19C, 20

The poem "Footprints in the Sand" is both famous and impressive. In that imaginary scene, the writer comes to understand that <u>God's footprints</u> were always there, even when the sand recorded only one set of them. He was at that point carrying His child.

This picture, however, is a different one. The image here is also one of sand that has only one set of footprints, but this time they are our own, and not God's! It is a reminder that there are times in life when God's people have no visible evidence of His Presence, but that the inability to see a set of <u>*divine footprints*</u> does not change a thing. He is still there, and He is still leading. Faith tells us so!

I would never say that <u>God's footprints</u> were nowhere to be seen in this dark valley through which He has been leading me. In spite of the darkness, I can see them faintly, and sometimes even clearly!

John Peterson expressed it well when he penned the words,

> Jesus led me all the way,
> Led me step by step each day;
> I will tell the saints and angels
> As I lay my burdens down,
> "Jesus led me all the way."

One of the verses of that song is especially persistent:

> If God should let me there review
> The winding paths of earth I knew,
> It would be proven clear and true —
> Jesus led me all the way.

Yes, even when *God's footprints are not seen*, He is still leading His people. The darkness can totally obscure the sight of *His footprints*, but it cannot erase His Presence. He has chosen to make His Presence "felt" rather than "seen," and there is infinite wisdom in that decision.

. . . though Your footprints were not seen, You led Your people . . .

WEARY WITH SORROW

"I weep with grief; my heart is heavy with sorrow; encourage and
cheer me with your words."
"My soul is weary with sorrow. Strengthen me according
to Thy word."
PSALM 119:28 THE LIVING BIBLE AND NIV

A *weary soul — a heavy heart.* Those words aptly describe
my feelings! The Psalmist paints a realistic, even if
morbid, picture.

But he does not stop with such morbidity. He wisely cries
out to the Lord, *Strengthen me! Encourage me! Cheer me!*

God does all of that. *He strengthens and encourages and cheers.*
The *strengthening* enables me to endure my grief. The
encouragement helps me to rise above it. The *cheering* empowers
me to triumph over it.

It seems to me that cheer is the opposite of grief. I had
very little of it in the beginning, but that is changing,
according to His word. My dear Father keeps His word.
Never have I needed the proof of that more than in these
oppressing days while traversing earth's darkest and deepest
valley.

I acknowledge, Lord, that my heart is very *weary with sorrow*. I thank You for these three words You have given me today: *encourage, strengthen, cheer*. They have become strong pillars that will bolster my sagging spirit.

A *heavy he*art and a *weary soul* do not sound spiritual. I cannot deny that there are moments when my spirituality is quite low. I don't like others to know that, so I wear my mask. But I cannot hide anything from You, and I don't even try.

You know me through and through. You know what I need and in Your great love You stoop to meet that need, lovingly, graciously and even generously. Take heart, my heavy heart! Rise up, my weary soul! Your God, all-mighty and all-loving, has made a provision for You that you must not miss!   *

DESERT PRAISE

"Then they came to Elim, where there were twelve springs and seventy palm trees, and they camped there near the water. The whole Israelite community set out from Elim and came to the Desert of Sin . . . in the desert the whole community grumbled against Moses and Aaron . . . 'You have brought us out into this desert to starve this entire assembly to death.' . . . So Moses and Aaron said to all the Israelites, 'In the evening you will know that it was the LORD who brought you out of Egypt, and in the morning you will see the glory of the LORD, because he has heard your grumbling against him . . . You will know it was the LORD . . . You are not grumbling against us, but against the LORD.' "

EXODUS 17:27; 16:1-8

T he Israelites complained that Moses and Aaron had brought them into this desert. But they were so very wrong! Without question, it was the Lord Who had done that.

I must never duplicate their error. When I enter one of the "deserts" of life, and I'm tempted to murmur and complain, I must remember that it was the Lord Who brought me into that desert, just as surely as on other occasions He has brought me to my "Elims" with their springs and palm trees.

I thoroughly enjoy the oasis experiences in life. Springs and palms are exotic and refreshing. I can enjoy sitting in the shade of a palm tree, drinking cool water from a spring. There is something both relaxing and rejuvenating about that kind of experience. But life is not made up of one Elim after another. There are deserts as well. I do not want a single one of them to be called *The Desert of Sin* in my life. All too easily deserts can become places where sin thrives in the sandy soil. Grumbling and complaining grow well in desert sand.

By God's grace I will recognize and acknowledge that it was God Who led me there. When I find myself in a desert — in the midst of one of my "dry" spells — I will continue to glorify my Lord, and praise Him even when the hot sand burns my tender toes.

COMING SOON!

"Behold, I am coming soon!"
"Behold, I am coming soon!"
REVELATION 22:7A, 12A

T wice in a span of only five verses this announcement is boldly proclaimed. I thrill to hear this trumpet call from the Revelation Mountain Range.

Only nine verses from the very end of the Bible we have this twice-stated promise, and it is not the last time it is proclaimed. In the next to the last verse of this final chapter, He reaffirms, *"Yes, I am coming soon,"* to which the Apostle John replies, "Amen. Come quickly, Lord Jesus."

No one who ever lived before us had more reason to expect the fulfillment of that promise than we do. The " . . . signs of His coming multiply; morning light breaks in the eastern sky." I don't have to be an expert in Bible prophecy to realize that wars and rumors of wars are signs of the end time. We have lots of those. The Bible predicts that frequent earthquakes will cause the earth to tremble. California alone has recently experienced multiplied thousands of tremors large enough to be recorded on the Richter scale. The Bible predicts that evil will "flourish" on the earth. Even in our own "Christian" country evil is rampant.

What a change the coming of the Lord Jesus will effect! "Satan's dominion will then be o'er; sorrow and sighing shall be no more." The prospect of that painless, sorrowless, sinless day is most appealing. I thrill to read the words of the Lord Jesus that John recorded for me, *"Behold I am coming soon!"* It is very easy for me to add my voice to John's, exclaiming with excitement, "Amen! Come quickly, Lord Jesus."

To his prayer I add, *"And while I wait, Lord, please keep that blessed hope burning brightly within me, sustaining and encouraging me, uplifting me when the waves of grief crash over me, threatening to inundate my spirit."*

"Behold, I am coming soon!"

"Behold, I am coming soon!"

IN THE COURSE OF TIME

"In the course of time, David defeated the Philistines and subdued them . . . "
I CHRONICLES 18:1A

"Time is a great healer!" people say to me, as if this were some profound declaration. The truth of the matter is that time itself doesn't heal a thing. It *takes* time for healing, but time does not *bring* the healing. My honey's experience makes that very clear. The longer our battle continued, the worse her condition became. Nor will time heal me — God will!

My own attitudes can help to shorten the time it takes. My scheduled activities will contribute. The tenor of my meditations will make a difference. The willingness of my heart to be healed will facilitate my healing. But time itself will not be able to make much of a boast as to its contribution to the process.

I know people who are not fully healed after decades of grieving. I know of others who are beautifully whole after only a few years. My situation will be my very own, and not patterned after someone else's. My sweetheart was unique.

178

My relationship to her was unique. I am unique. The ingredients going into this hot oven are not quite the same as in any one else's.

That does not mean there are no similarities. I can learn from others. I can profit from reading books on grief. I can be blessed by talking to someone who has walked this same painful trail before me. A grief support group may be used by God to facilitate my healing. And then, *in His time*, I shall be healed.

Yes, *in the course of time*, I shall defeat these Philistines that have oppressed me. But it won't be time that does it. It will be God Himself, with my cooperation.

The course of time will bring many joys, in fact. In the course of time my Savior will return to this earth to catch me up into His presence — and hers! *In the course of time* the Prince of Peace will bring peace to an earth characterized by wars and rumors of wars. *In the course of time* this earthly assignment will be completed. Tears and heartache and suffering and separation will be a forgotten past!

TRANSCENDENT PEACE

". . . the peace of God, which transcends all understanding, will guard your
hearts and your minds in Christ Jesus."
PHILIPPIANS 4:7

What a blessing is *transcendent peace!* There are times when peace does not come naturally; in fact, it is downright unnatural. Yet God provides a sweet, beautiful peace that the world can only marvel at. I think of two hymns that eloquently speak of the *transcendent peace* of God:

Far away in the depths of my spirit tonight
    Flows a melody sweeter than psalm;
In celestial-like strains it unceasing falls
    O'er my soul like an infinite calm.

What a treasure I have in this wonderful peace
    Buried deep in the heart of my soul,
So secure that no power can mine it away
    While the years of eternity roll.

I am resting tonight in this wonderful peace,
    Resting sweetly in Jesus' control;

For I'm kept from all danger by night and by day
And His glory is flooding my soul.

Peace, peace, wonderful peace,
    Coming down from the Father above.
Sweep over my spirit forever, I pray,
    In fathomless billows of love.

W. D. Cornell

It really is a peace that transcends all understanding. There are aspects of this peace that are quite phenomenal. The question and answer structure of another hymn reflects the wonder of it all:

Peace, perfect peace, in this dark world of sin?
    The blood of Jesus whispers "peace" within.
Peace, perfect peace, with sorrows surging 'round?
    On Jesus' bosom naught but calm is found.
Peace, perfect peace, with loved ones far away?
    In Jesus' keeping we are safe, and they.
Peace, perfect peace, our future all unknown?
    Jesus we know, and He is on the throne.
Peace, perfect peace, death shadowing us and ours?
    Jesus has vanquished death and all its powers.

Edward H. Bickersteth

Yes, the peace of God *is* a peace that transcends all understanding. It is a peace that thrives in climates where one would never expect it to exist, let alone thrive. It is a *transcendent peace*!

BE STILL

"Do not be afraid. Stand still and you will see the deliverance the LORD will bring you today. The Egyptians you see today you will never see again. The LORD will fight for you; you need only to <u>be still</u>."
EXODUS 14:13,14

"You need only to <u>be still</u>.*"* There's a sweet, quiet power inherent in stillness that the world knows nothing about, primarily because it knows nothing about the nature of God. The times are bustling, brash and brazenly boisterous. Consequently, we are not as familiar with the "Blessed Quietness" spoken of in one of our gospel songs as we ought to be. The evil triumvirate of Hurry, Flurry and Worry are much better known and certainly more popular.

"<u>Be still</u> and know that I am God," the psalmist Korah wrote. And so beautifully, the twentieth century psalmist, Mrs. Hal Buckner, expressed it:

> That He is God, *<u>be still</u>* and know,
> > Though storm-swept be your weary soul,
> > > *<u>Your deepest grief to Him is woe,</u>*
> > And over all He has control.

Though shattered hopes surround you still,
Though dark and rugged is your way,
Know this: for you a Father's will,
Preordains all things day by day.

No depth of storm nor strength of gale,
Can move you from your place secure;
His power o'er these shall still prevail,
His boundless love shall still endure.

Chorus

Be still and know. *Be still and know,*
That He is God, *be still* and know.
He sees and feels your deepest woe,
That He is God, *be still* and know.

There is a profound beauty and inconceivable strength in the simple admonition, *You do not need to be afraid, stand firm, you need only to be still.* *

HE REACHED DOWN

*"He reached down from on high and took hold of me; He drew me
out of deep waters."*
PSALM 18:16

When the artist painted a giant hand *reaching down* out
of a stormy sky toward a turbulent sea in which a
person was sinking, he so graphically depicted the promise in
this verse.

More dramatic yet is the literal fulfillment of this promise
when I find myself threatened by deep waters, as I do now,
and I experience a lifting up by means of that huge, powerful
hand of God.

God has surely helped me. He has given me grace for each
day. He has renewed my strength on more than one occasion.
He has brought one serendipity after another into my life,
such as notes of caring encouragement from unexpected
sources and the assurances of regular prayer support from
people I didn't know cared that much. He has helped me not
to cast away my confidence, even in the midst of deep, deep
grieving.

Deep waters never did frighten Him like they do me. He walked on the troubled waters, putting them beneath His feet. I worry about their going over my head! It is well for me to slip my hand into His and enjoy the feeling of having all these troubles beneath my feet as well. They may not be gone, but whether they are beneath my feet or over my head makes a world of difference.

He reached down! What a beautiful condescension! It amazes me to think that His mighty hand *reaches down* to this small house on my little street, right into my life because He knows how desperately I need Him. There He lifts me up, encourages me, and repeats to me His loving promises.

I need to be more conscious both of the strength and of the presence of that uplifting hand, and less conscious of the viciousness of this storm. Then I will enjoy a peace in the midst of the storm that will be a good testimony to the loving faithfulness of my Lord.

He reached down from on high and took hold of me; He drew me out of deep waters.

A PREPARED PLACE

"I am going . . . to prepare a place for you. And if I go and prepare a place for you, I will come back and take you to be with me that you also may be where I am."

JOHN 14:2, 3

How ever can my earthbound imagination rise to picture in any adequate manner the place the Lord Jesus is preparing for me? It must be beautiful beyond my wildest imagination. He has had two thousand years to perfect it with details that are so extravagantly elegant that I could never conceive of them prior to experiencing them.

Even now the most impressive things on earth are not man-made, but are what we call "wonders of nature." The roaring falls of Niagara and Iguazu and Victoria cause man to view them with unbridled awe. The grandeur of the well-named Grand Canyon cannot be adequately described — they must be experienced. The marvel of El Altar and Cayambe and Sangai as they scrape the skies of Ecuador with their perpetually snowcapped peaks cannot be fully depicted by word or photo. The miles and miles of tulips in Holland, the carpet of grapes along the Rhine, the splendor of the towering Yungfrau and of Mount Pilatus in Switzerland — all of these are God-made, not man-made. They are only prototypes of what I shall experience and take delight in when I see what He has prepared for me up there. And far better than all of that will be the pure enjoyment of being with Him whom my soul adores. What an ecstasy of joy that will be!

My dear sweetheart has preceded me there. For her it was far more than a release from her frail body. It was a glorious rendezvous with Him whom her soul had so deeply loved. Someday I shall join her there. Together we will contemplate the wonders of His handiwork on a far grander scale than we have done here. Together we will worship the One Who gave us such a rich and rewarding life down here, as well as our eternal, glorious, abundant life up there.

This revelation of the current activity of the Lord Jesus and this promise of His return to get me bring both excitement and a surge of joy to my grieving heart.　　＊

GREET THE DAWN WITH SONG

"Rouse yourself, my soul! Arise . . . let us greet the dawn with song!"
PSALM 57:8 THE LIVING BIBLE

This morning I heard myself humming! It was such a pleasure to realize that I was able to *greet the dawn with a song*. I had no heartfelt song for awhile. This valley does not echo with sounds of singing, by any means. The more familiar sounds have been *sniffles* and *sighs*. Today — *a song!*

I even stopped to listen to what I was humming, and thought of the words that go with the melody that was breaking forth to *greet the dawn*. It was an oldie that I have not heard for years. I could only remember the first three words of the song, so I looked it up in an old <u>Singspiration</u> songbook entitled "50 Sacred Favorites." It was so old that it had a $1.00 price tag on it! The song:

> Beyond the sunset, O blissful morning,
> When with our Savior heav'n is begun;
> Earth's toiling ended, O glorious dawning,
> Beyond the sunset, when day is done.

Beyond the sunset, O glad reunion
With our dear loved ones who've gone before;
In that fair homeland we'll know no parting,
Beyond the sunset forevermore!

Virgil P. Brock / Blanche Kerr Brock

While searching for the lyrics of that one, I came across another old one so familiar to me and so appropriate to today's text:

I had no song and life was dreary,
No hope had I to which to cling;
Until one day I heard my Savior say,
"My child rejoice, *rejoice and sing!*"

Chorus
The Lord gave me a song.
The Lord gave me a song!
The clouds have been scattered,
The sunlight appears.
The rainbow of promise
Now shines through my tears.
The Lord gave me a song.
The Lord gave me a song!
He banished my sadness
And filled me with gladness,

Unknown

Yes, I can *greet the dawn with song* now, because the Lord has given me a song — implanted in a heart that earlier was too grieved to sing. *

INCREDIBLY GREAT POWER

"I pray that you will begin to understand how incredibly great His power is to help those who believe Him."
EPHESIANS 1:19 THE LIVING BIBLE

H*is "incredibly great power!"* That's what Paul calls it. It is a power so great that it is beyond my comprehension.

Once in awhile I catch a glimpse of it, as when God does something special which is above and beyond what man can take credit for. Then my heart eagerly responds, "Yes, God's power is most certainly *incredibly great!* There is nothing too hard for the Lord!" The truth is that the scope of His power extends outward forever, like the universe itself. For years man has been grappling with the concept of an ever-expanding universe that has no outward limitations. It is a theory that is too big for his little mind.

I live in an *incredibly great* universe, the creation of an *incredibly great* God by exercising His *incredibly great power*. But the marvel of this text is that God says His limitless power is exercised on my behalf! This verse could so smoothly have stopped after saying, *I pray that you will begin to understand how incredibly great His power is.* But it does not stop there; it goes on to read, . . . *to help those who believe Him.*

That incredibly great power is there *for me!* I must permit nothing to rob me of that truth — not grief, nor loneliness, nor weakness, nor fear, nor life's storms, nor any other trial the enemy may devise.

God is God! *His incredibly great power* has never been diminished even minutely by exercising it. Nor has it been affected one iota by man's attempts to limit and define Him. I will trust Him to use that power on my behalf in each new day in whatever way He chooses. I will face this day expecting Him to exhibit *His incredibly great power* — perhaps even in ways that will please me as well as mightily glorify Him.

I pray that you will begin to understand how incredibly great His power is to help those who believe him.

SPIRITUAL BLESSINGS

*"Praise be to the God and Father of our Lord Jesus Christ, who has
blessed us . . . with every spiritual blessing . . ."*
EPHESIANS 1:3

My heart spontaneously responds with praise when I
meditate upon the multitude of *spiritual blessings* with
which God has enriched my life. I am very well-to-do in the
things of the Spirit.

The value of my eternal salvation is inestimable. The
beauty of my fellowship with God, which has been restored
to me, can only be fully experienced, not adequately
described. The awesome privilege of being a joint-heir with
Jesus Christ staggers my mind. The priceless gift of eternal
life defies the ability of my finite mind to comprehend; how
can the finite comprehend the infinite?

I praise the Lord Who has so richly blessed me. His
wisdom and knowledge are boundless, and He has generously
given some to me, for we are told that "Christ Jesus . . . has
become for us wisdom from God." His power is limitless and
He has placed that power at my disposal through such
fabulous promises as, "I will do anything you ask in my name,

so that the Son may bring glory to the Father. You may ask me for anything in my name and I will do it (John 14:13,14).

His love is incomparable and He has lavishly showered it upon me, loving me with an everlasting love. His sovereignty coupled with His beneficent nature guarantees me that everything shall continue to work together for my good — eternally!

Yes, He has blessed me with all spiritual blessings; and even if I, too (as did my loved one) were to develop a deficiency in the area of physical blessings, I can remind myself that physical problems are temporary. I have a brand-new body coming that cannot be touched by earth's diseases and will not deteriorate with age. How rich I am — how very rich I am!

Praise be to the God and Father of our Lord Jesus Christ, who has blessed us . . . with every spiritual blessing . . . "

LOVE-STRENGTH COMBO

"In Your unfailing love You will lead the people You have redeemed. In Your strength You will guide them to Your holy dwelling."
EXODUS 15:13

This verse is worthy of memorization, yet it is not one of the standard ones God's people tend to zero in on.

God's guidance is spoken of twice in this verse. First it is coupled with unfailing *love*. Then it is linked with His great *strength*. What a combination!

God's *strength* is activated on my behalf by His unfailing *love*. That's a win/win situation. There is no losing, ever, when my all-powerful God, knowing every detail of my existence by virtue of His omniscience, decides to intervene in my life because of His unfailing, unlimited love.

A sincere "Hallelujah!" wells up in my heart as I think about this. God paid a great price for me. He is not all that different from me in that He wants to preserve the product of His lavish expenditure. I don't think of myself as a "pearl of great price," yet He implies that I am, for I am being changed into Christ's own likeness!

Basking in the warmth of another's love is a beautiful thing. My sweetheart and I loved each other deeply, sincerely and consistently. Yet our love pales in significance when compared with the love with which He has loved me!

O perfect love, all human loves transcending!
Lowly (I) kneel in prayer before Thy throne,
That (I may bask in)
The love which knows no ending,
(Thou hast forever made me all Thine own!).

Dorothy Gurney

God's *love* combined with His unlimited *strength* exercised on my behalf is both a powerful and comforting privilege. My heart is splendidly uplifted as I read and meditate upon this forceful, stimulating, love-prompted text.

In Your unfailing love You will lead the people You have redeemed. In Your strength You will guide them to Your holy dwelling."

I MUST TELL JESUS

I must tell Jesus all of my trials;
I cannot bear (this grieving) alone;
In my distress He kindly will help me;
He ever loves and cares for His own.
I must tell Jesus, I must tell Jesus,
I cannot bear (this sorrow) alone;
I must tell Jesus, I must tell Jesus.
Jesus can help me, Jesus alone.

After quite a few months of grieving, some of my well-meaning friends think I should be healing by this time. They don't speak from experience! My few friends who have been through it never suggest that I am progressing too slowly. They know better!

Oh, no one actually says anything specific about my slowness to heal, but every once in awhile my suspicions are confirmed by something they do say. It may be that I am just paranoid, I don't know.

I do have a definite impression that there are very few who want me to talk about my sweetheart. Their lives continue on as usual. The fact of her demise does not affect them as it does me. I don't expect it to. I am the one who has suffered the amputation and I must adjust to my new world without a lot of empathy on their part.

But there is One! To Him I can go any hour of the day or night. I can repeat any memories of my honey frequently without being misjudged or rebuffed. He knows that I cherish those precious memories and take comfort in reiterating them. He doesn't think I am coming down with Alzheimer's or slipping into some kind of temporary insanity when I rehearse them frequently. He loved her too! More dearly than I do! So, I enjoy talking to Jesus about her. The depth of the love we both have for her is something He and I have in common.

Yes, I'm "grieving o'er a (spouse) departed, and I will "*tell it to Jesus — tell it to Jesus.*" I've " . . . no other, such a friend or brother," so I'll just "*tell it to Jesus* alone."

A HEART AT PEACE

"A heart at peace gives life to the body . . ."
PROVERBS 14:30

S omewhere I read an article that asserted that the first six to nine months are critical in the physical well-being of the grief-stricken person. The article stated that many bereaved persons develop physical problems probably precipitated by their grieving.

I don't want that to happen to me. My sweetheart would not want that to happen, either. I must pay attention to God's formula for health and wholeness during that critical period: *a heart at peace!*

God gave me and my honey an amazing peace and contentment in the midst of our protracted trial. What a wonderful gift that was! I am sure He does not intend that I should lack that same peace now.

This verse reveals a side effect of the heart that enjoys a God-given peace. *Life itself* is said to be a by-product. God's medications and stimulants to health are so different from man's. In another verse the Lord tells us that a merry heart is good medicine (Proverbs 14:22). Here I am told that *a peaceful* _heart gives life to the body._ So then, anything that deepens my sense of peace or brings rejoicing to my heart becomes good therapy for me and a powerful medicine.

This truth is the antithesis of the way stress brings on disease. The body is weakened by stress; it is strengthened by peace. Stress opens the door to disease; peace closes it.

Can peace and sorrow live together? Amazingly, yes! After H. G. Spafford's four daughters had drowned, he wrote the hymn that has blessed so many hearts from that time on, "When peace like a river attendeth my way; when sorrows like sea billows roll, whatever my lot, Thou has taught me to say, 'It is well. It is well, with my soul.' " He mentions peace and sorrows in the same sentence!

My prayer, then, is for a heart that continues at peace even during this extension to the Valley of the Shadow of Death. Yes, dear Lord, please give to me the peace that passes understanding — the peace that does not come naturally to a broken heart.

A heart at peace gives life to the body . . .

IT'S ALL RIGHT

" 'It's all right,' she said, . . . 'everything is all right . . .' "
II KINGS 4:23C

There is no more amazing statement of faith than this one to be found anywhere in the Bible. In the midst of her heartbreak and grief this Shunammite woman could make firm statements of faith like this! If ever there were an illustration of "denial" this would be it (for analysts who like to try to explain away such faith-statements).

Even in the midst of my own grief, I too can say by faith, *It's all right!* I can say it because I know my Heavenly Father has not lost control, and He will bring me through this torturous, lonely valley in triumph. I will heal. I will not be overcome by these painful feelings. I will not drown in my tears. I will emerge triumphant — in His time. Those are certainties that faith boldly expresses.

I want to be more like this Shunammite woman. To anyone who asks how I am doing, I want to be able to say, *It's all right! Everything is all right!* Even when my heart is still broken and bleeding, I can say these things as faith statements and not as current weather reports.

It has been quite a few months now. The periods of deep grieving come less frequently. They do not last as long. This does not mean that I have forgotten her. Her star will always be uniquely fixed in my sky! It just means that I am healing. I can walk taller now. I can better tolerate the heartrending hymns at church. I can laugh a little. I can sometimes find myself spontaneously humming. I can plan future travels and events with a measure of joyful anticipation. The pleasure capacity is making a comeback, and that's most welcome.

It's all right! *Yes, everything is all right* — or at least I have confidence that it will be, as time passes. My loving Lord has never abandoned me, and He never will. He has walked with me through this dark segment of the Valley of the Shadow of Death. I will fear no evil. *Everything is all right!*

My Faithful Shepherd

". . . the God who has been <u>my Shepherd</u> all my life to this day . . ."
GENESIS 48:15B

Jacob had lived 147 years when he said that! That warm, confident statement was backed by more experience of trusting than I can ever hope to have.

David is credited with the analogy of the Lord being our Shepherd as the twenty-third Psalm so beautifully states. Yet, long before he penned that poetic psalm, Jacob had called his Lord, . . . *the God who has been <u>my Shepherd</u> all my life to this day . . ."*

David spelled out the implications thoroughly, including lying down in green pastures, being led beside still waters, being protected by the rod and the staff of the Shepherd, etc. Jacob just lets the primary thought stand out boldly, without elaboration. Both men were sheepherders. Both knew the importance of the shepherd's actions to the well-being of the sheep.

God has been *<u>my Shepherd</u>, too, all my life to this very day.* He will continue the faithful, loving care He has given right up to this point. I must never doubt that. When I look to the future and have concerns as to what may happen to me, I am failing to remember that the Good Shepherd — *my faithful Shepherd* — is not changeable. He even takes pride in the fact that He is unchangeable. He changes not. His compassions, they fail not. As He has been, He forever will be. A month from now, a year from now, ten years from now, or on the very last day of my life, when that comes, I will still be able to refer to my Heavenly Father, along with Jacob, as *the God Who has been my Shepherd all my life to this day.*

How privileged I am to have a Gentle Shepherd Who looks out for my every need. I am richly blessed, and I say worshipfully, "Bless the Lord, O my soul, and all that is within me, bless His holy name!"

Without question, *God has been my Shepherd all my life to this very day!*

A STRANGER ON EARTH

"I am a stranger on earth . . ."
DEUTERONOMY 33:27A

There are times when it would be easy for me to slip into self-pity as I recognize that my home has now become just a house. It was our beautiful relationship that transformed these walls into a home. With my sweetheart gone, these are familiar walls, but no longer my *home*.

So, dear Lord, I need the perspective this verse provides. I need to remember that I am *a stranger here*, and it is quite normal for the earth not to seem like my "home" as I await my own call to my real "home."

> I am *a stranger here*, within a foreign land,
>   My home is far away, upon a golden strand
> Ambassador to be of realms beyond the sea,
>   I'm here on business for my King.
>
> Elijah T. Cassel

That's not just poetic expression. It has a biblical basis. Both today's verse and one in the New Testament substantiate that line of thinking: "All these people . . .

204

admitted that they were aliens and *strangers on earth* . . . they were longing for a better country — a heavenly one." And who were "these people" referred to here? They were the ones who were living by faith, for this verse is found in the midst of the beautiful "Faith Chapter" (Hebrews 11:13-16).

So, instead of wallowing in self-pity that my "home" has become a "house," I shall long for a better country — a heavenly one. And, while I live in this "house," I shall, by the grace of God, see to it that from it there shall regularly flow words of comfort and encouragement to others. I refuse to become "housebound" by negativism. Even though this world is not my home, it shall be my parish. I will do my best to dispatch words of comfort to others. I will, in every way I can, bring cheer and blessing to those in need of it, so that I am making the most of my newly defined existence. In this way, I will be pleasing to the One Who decided to take my loved one — and leave me. I am here for a purpose. Though I am *a stranger here*, I am determined that this stranger shall be a blessing.

COVENANT KEEPER

". . . our God . . . keeps his covenant of love . . ."
NEHEMIAH 9:32

O h yes, He does! Indeed He does! I have benefited from His loving faithfulness repeatedly. How sincerely I praise Him!

"I will never leave you nor forsake you" is one of His comforting promises. I can say with deep feeling, "He never has!" Through all the difficult terrain I have encountered, God has been there by my side. He has faithfully guided my footsteps, lest I dash my foot against a stone. He has *kept His covenant of love.*

"I will instruct you and teach you in the way that you should go," is another of His clear promises. I can look back upon specific guidance that was incredibly detailed, and I am thrilled. Again I say, He has *kept His covenant of love.*

"When you pass through the waters they will not overflow you, and when you pass through the fire, it will not burn you," He promised me; and though I have been through both "floods" and "fire", I am still walking in victory. I was not drowned. I was not burned. He has graciously _kept His covenant_ of love.

He promised to "supply all my need out of His riches in glory by Christ Jesus." Generously, and even copiously, He has done that. I have had need of nothing. Even our heavy medical expenses were so faithfully cared for. He has bountifully _kept His covenant_ of love.

I don't know all that lies ahead of me. Just thinking about it frightens me sometimes. But this I do know, and upon this truth I must continually dwell: Our faithful Lord is One Who _keeps his covenant_ of love. He has in the past — He will in the future, irrespective of what that future includes.

"I will fear no evil!" Why should I, when my God is such a dependable _Covenant Keeper?_

. . . our God . . . keeps his covenant of love . . .

TAKE COURAGE!

"When Asa heard these words . . . he took courage."
II CHRONICLES 15:8A

May it please You, Lord, to let the thoughts in these
devotionals bring courage to fainting hearts. You did
that for Elaine and me while we walked hand in hand through
the darkest valley of our life. You can do it now for the
multitudes who find that the Valley of the Shadow of Death
does not end with the death of their loved one.

No matter what anyone says, this Valley of the Shadow of
Death is an extremely difficult one. It is filled with agonies,
fears, heartbreaks, shattered dreams, uncertainties, steep
ascents (and descents!), briars and thorns, clouds, rain,
precipices, boulders that frighten and stones that trip,
loneliness, questions, tears and weakness. I am not
exaggerating — I have been there!

But so have You, Lord Jesus! That's the beauty of it. You
brought to me comfort beyond anything I have ever
experienced before, encouragement that was supernatural,
hope when there was no earthly hope, reassurance when my
faith lagged and I had none left, rays of sunlight on some of

the darkest days and in the midst of terrible storms, promises that never failed, a fresh renewing when it seemed as if I had exhausted my store of endurance. Your staff comforted me. Your love overshadowed and warmed me. You gave me the ability to see the flowers that grow in that dark valley! I learned that some flowers do grow in that gloomy atmosphere, and even thrive there! You gave me immunity to the dashing of my foot against any stones (Psalm 91:12). You provided Kleenex to wipe away my tears, Band-Aids to cover the briar scratches, vitamins to pep me up again, Visine for my red eyes, and warm clothing when the climate was so bitterly cold. You provided spiritual armor, including the helmet of salvation, the breastplate of righteousness, and the preparation of peace. But Your best gift of all was the sustaining power of Your incomparable Presence ("Thou art with me!").

Yes,

I have been through the Valley of Weeping,
The Valley of Sorrow and pain,
But the God of all Comfort was with me,
At hand to uphold and sustain.

I, too, will *hear these words . . . and take courage.*

209

OTHER BOOKS BY
CHARLES W. SHEPSON

How to Know God's Will
How to Rise Above Depression
To Stephanie and Steven, With Love, From Grampa
Quiet Miracles I, II, III
Hidden Manna
Hidden Manna for the Caregiver
Hidden Manna For the Hungry Heart
A Heart for Imbabura
The Ultimate Intimacy

- -

How to Know God's Will is very practical and useful for those who are earnestly wanting to determine God's will. The new, revised edition is now available. There are 47,000 copies in print.

How to Rise Above Depression is a study of the methods God used to cure Elijah of his deep depression. It has helpful information for all who suffer from depression.

To Stephanie and Steven, With Love, From Grampa is an autobiography filled with amazing accounts of answers to prayer written especially for the author's grandchildren. Note: See also the description of *Quiet Miracles*.

Quiet Miracles I is a revision of the *Grampa* book described previously, with additional stories added. It is the first book in the autobiographic series, *God is not Silent.*

Quiet Miracles II and *Quiet Miracles III* are additional vignettes in the autobiographic series, *God is not Silent,* filled with amazing accounts of answers to prayer.

Hidden Manna is comprised of daily devotionals with a positive tone to encourage those who have a life-threatening illness.

Hidden Manna for the Caregiver contains ninety-nine devotionals for persons who are caregivers for a loved one. It is designed to strengthen them for their difficult task.

Hidden Manna for the Hungry Heart contains more than 100 brief devotionals for all Christians. The devotions are based on verses from a dozen translations and paraphrases.

A Heart for Imbabura is a stirring missionary biography of Evelyn Rychner, who served in Ecuador. The fabulous breakthrough God gave among the Otavalo Indians is thrilling.

The Ultimate Intimacy is a book with chapters arranged in an ever-deepening level of intimacy, culminating in the final chapter with the revelation of what the author considers the ultimate intimacy to be. It is important to read these chapters consecutively, even though each chapter stands on its own.

Books may be ordered from:

Fairhaven Ministries
2198 Ripshin Mountain Rd.
Roan Mountain, TN 37687

or through the following website:
www.shieldsgroup.com/books